# MANTRAS:
## A Musical Path to Peace

Henry Marshall, Ph.D.

Mantras are magical sounds that protect, heal, and liberate. In the mystic traditions of the East they have been used for thousands of years to rejuvenate, to achieve noble intentions, and to reach inner peace. In daily Western life, mantras can help heal the body, relax the mind, quiet the emotions, and open the heart. Ultimately, they provide a raft across the ocean of discovery to the joy of liberation.

This book is intended to encourage sincere seekers and curious skeptics to explore the mysterious transformative power of mantras. Woven into the narrative is almost everything you might want to know about mantras as tools for spiritual development and personal transformation. At its deepest level, this little book provides a map that can help you discover the magic of mantras.

Henry Marshall, Ph.D. is a Western-trained clinical psychologist, wise in the ways of Eastern philosophies, healing, and meditation. He and Rickie Moore are life partners and co-therapists in the Inner Peace Playshops. His extraordinary therapeutic skills and his heartfelt simplicity awaken even skeptical people to the pleasure and power of chanting mantras. Together with the musicians of the Playshop Family, he has recorded *Mantras: Magical Songs of Power* (1994), *Mantras II: To Change Your World* (1995), and *Mantras III: A Little Bit of Heaven* (1998).

*Henry Marshall, Ph.D.*

# *Mantras*
## *A Musical Path to Peace*

**Bluestar Communications®**

Woodside, California

Published by:
Bluestar Communications
44 Bear Glenn
Woodside, CA 94062
Tel: 800-6-Bluestar (650-851-5880)


Cover design: Petra Michel
Layout: Petra Michel

First printing 1999
ISBN: 1-885394-34-9

*Library of Congress Cataloging-in-Publication Data*

Marshall, Henry, 1949-
    Mantras : a musical path to peace / Henry Marshall.
        p. cm.
    Includes bibliographical references and index.
    ISBN 1-885394-34-9
    1. Hindu mantras--Therapeutic use. 2. Psychotherapy--Religious
aspects--Hinduism. 3. Psychotherapists--United States--Biography.
4. Spiritual biography--United States. 5. Marshall, Henry, 1949-.
      I. Title.
BL1236.38.M39  1999
291.3' 7--dc21                          98-43115
                                                     CIP

Nothing herein is presented or recommended as diagnosis or prescription or as a substitute for medical care.

This book is dedicated to sincere seekers of truth.

Printed in China

# *Acknowledgments*

This book exists because of the trust and support of many wonderful people. My deep thanks especially go to the following great souls.

≈ *Rickie Moore*, my darling Satya, leads many roles in my life: as beloved life-partner, soul mate, guide, and companion in this world, she is truly the answer to a heartfelt prayer; as collaborator, co-therapist, and co-producer, she is co-creator of all my endeavors.

≈ *Satguru Sant Keshavadas* (1934-1997) awakened the sound of mantras in my soul, and blessed me to spread them into the world.

≈ *Adano Ley* (1924-1989) shared his deep wisdom and healing powers, and started me on the path of love and service.

≈ *Steven Fenberg* and *Albert Rutz* very generously gave their time, creativity, and editorial assistance to help this book become more coherent and accessible. *Elena Brentel* and *Wolfgang Suttner* read the drafts several times, gave loving feedback, and helped the book find its form. *Mélisande Buitenkamp* worked long and carefully on the musical notation. *Werner and Rosalie Kubny, Adrienne Lueders*, and *Andreas Pfeuti* all helped correct the music along the way. *Petra Michel* of Bluestar Communications and *David Grabijn* and *Frank van der Velden* of Oreade Music had the vision, flexibility, and perseverance that enabled mantra recordings to accompany the text of this book.

The mantra chanters and magical musicians of the *Playshop Family*[1] have supported my spirit and given me the courage to bring the mantras out into the world. They encouraged me to teach them mantras, provided over a hundred angels of music who made it possible to record them, and insisted that I write this book.

*Henry Marshall, Amsterdam, October 1998*

---

[1] Refers to the network of individuals in numerous countries who have participated in workshops led by Rickie Moore and Henry Marshall—Inner Peace Playshops—five day gatherings of people who want to live more consciously and more joyfully. For more information contact the author at the address at the end of this book.

# *Contents*

# *Compact Disc*

| | |
|---|---|
| *Dhanyavad (for the joy of gratitude)* | 8.07 |
| *Jaya Jaya Devi Mata (for peace with the mother)* | 7.50 |
| *Om Srim Mahalakshmyai (for noble wealth)* | 13.53 |
| **total time** | 29.50 |

# *Introduction*

Mantras are magical sounds that protect, liberate, and heal. In the mystic traditions of the East they have been used for thousands of years to rejuvenate, to achieve noble intentions, and to reach inner peace. In daily Western life, mantras can help heal the body, relax the mind, quiet the emotions, and open the heart. Ultimately, they provide a raft across the sea of discovery to the joy of liberation.

In twenty years as a clinical psychologist and almost thirty years as a spiritual seeker, I have seen mantras transform and heal many emotional and psychosomatic disorders. Personally, I owe my joyous spiritual partnership, stable finances, rewarding life's work, and inner peace to the magic of mantras. The problem with such statements is that today, in this materialistic age, even the most inspired idea quickly becomes just another product competing in the marketplace. The challenge confronting the consumer culture of the West is to separate the helpful from the hype. Mantras are not immune to this confusion. To simply believe or not believe in the power of mantras is to miss the point. Results are the proof of their power.

This book is intended to encourage sincere seekers and curious skeptics to explore the mysterious transformative power of mantras. It is an autobiographical story of how mantras have guided me from being lonely, self-righteous, critical, and extremely obsessive-compulsive, to being loving, giving, tolerant—and only moderately obsessive-compulsive. It is a story of how a child became an adult, of how a student became a teacher. It gives reassurance that you do not have to renounce the world and chant for hours each day to use mantras to find peace and fulfillment. Woven into the narrative is almost everything you might want to know about mantras as tools for spiritual development and personal transformation. At its deepest level, this little book provides a map that can help you discover the magic of man-tras.

# I. Loneliness

*In the currently fashionable picture of the universe there is no place
for valid transcendental experience. Consequently those who have
what they regard as valid transcendental experiences are looked
upon with suspicion as being either lunatics or swindlers. To be a
mystic or visionary is no longer creditable.*

Aldous Huxley (1954)

## Southern-fried Karma

The mysteries of the East and the magic of mantras were worlds away from the farm
where I was raised in northwest Louisiana. While I was growing up, my old-line
family of the deep South was still struggling with the loss of the Civil War and lining
up on the wrong side of the budding civil rights movement. What remained of the
Marshall family's Allendale Plantation was an hour's drive over bumpy roads from
Shreveport, and a hundred years behind in time.

My mother, Mary Emily Barret, was brilliant and dramatic, not necessarily in that
order. She was the youngest child of a Louisiana family that prided itself on including a governor, a military hero, and numerous civic leaders. Mamma aspired to
greatness: high ideals at all times and perfecting the mundane whenever possible.
She was in her mid-thirties, working as secretary for the president of an oil com-

pany, and well known as an actress, when she met my father, who had just returned home from World War II.

My father was probably the gentlest man who ever served in the United States Army. Henry Marshall, Jr. was a southern gentleman to the core. He was the fourth generation, eldest son of a family that had settled Northwest Louisiana in the 1840s, and that had produced a number of teachers, Confederate statesmen, and farmers. When the Second World War broke out, he volunteered for military service and eventually commanded an anti-aircraft unit in the Aleutian Islands, where he suffered severe frostbite that left his face mildly palsied. As a result, in times of stress or exhaustion, one side of his face became curiously slack, and he would look tired and vulnerable. Although he was educated as an engineer and experienced as a surveyor, my father's dream was to run the farm where he had been raised.

Although Daddy was a couple of years younger than Mamma and several inches shorter, their friends and family thought they would make a perfect pair. Mamma was

Mamma, Daddy, and me

cultured and sophisticated; she fascinated my father. Daddy was courtly and persuasive; he convinced my mother that they could be happy living in the country. He built a house for her on the family land, and they moved in shortly before I was born.

I was given the name of my father and grandfather, a constant reminder that I should be gentlemanly, gracious, and refined. In our immediate family I was usually referred to as "Henry the third." However, when Mamma was angry she bellowed, "The Third!" and when affectionate, she called me "Prince." My father, on the other hand, almost always called me "Henny-boy." The black families who worked on our farm and in our house (and who were also our closest neighbors) called me "Little Mister Little Henry" whenever white adults were around. This was to differentiate me from my grandfather "Mr. Henry" and my father "Little Mr. Henry." My various names conjured up a confusing array of expectations. I felt more myself when I managed to get away from our house and across our quarter-mile front yard to play with the black children. Like spiritual seekers, actors, or gang members who adopt special names to express their aspirations and take distance from old identities, I visited the black families whenever I could, and in their world was simply "Henry."

I played for hours with the black children in front of their little cabin as the sun retreated behind the trees. When an early-evening breeze swayed the blue bottles hanging from the wisteria vines, they hummed with an eerie piping sound. Aunt Emma, the matriarch of the Ikner family, called them "Spirit catchers." "Folks say the spirits is drawed into the bottle by the sounds, and then cain't git out," she'd say solemnly, as if beginning an incantation. "I do not know as white folks believes that; but it's what the old folks say." If I was lucky and the rambunctious crowd of children was not too loud, she might tell a story. Once I found a blue bottle that had been buried, and asked Aunt Emma if I could hang it up to catch spirits. She told me if it was buried, "Better leave it, cause like as not it's full of spirits." Then she added with a chuckle, "You may be white, child, but your soul sho' nuff is black. Now you better git on home to yo' mamma." When I crossed the yard to my house, I missed the magic and closeness I was leaving.

As an infant, two black women who helped my mother cared for me. Their loving touch and soothing songs nurtured me and enabled me to trust them and their culture. As I grew older the passionate, rhythmic, sensual gospel songs of the field hands floated into my ears and sang on my lips. Somehow it just felt right to, "Lay down my burden, down by the riverside," rather than to go, "Onward Christian soldiers, marching as to war." The disapproval of my tight-lipped, lock-hipped Episcopalian family could not convince me otherwise. My increasing involvement with the black families did not please my parents, and probably contributed to their decision that the black families had to move off our property to land of their own about three-quarters of a mile away. At this distance, my friends and their other world were unreachable.

Spiritual education from my mother emphasized loving service more than religious practice. She revered Albert Schweitzer as a role model of a saintly man, who took his organ and medical kit to the jungle to help the Africans. She often referred to a bible passage engraved on a cup I got as an infant, "Do justly, love mercy, and walk humbly with thy God."[2] It had been given to me by Cousin Hollingsworth Barret, who she often told me was scholarly and ethical, and who she admired almost as much as Schweitzer.

I was a very skinny child and, despite being a good athlete and rather strong, I developed a body image of being not-big-and-strong-enough. One searing moment burned that impression into me when, at about eight years of age, I successfully wrestled with a difficult-to-open farm gate to let my mother drive through. In the car was my grandfather's second wife, whose full name always intrigued me: Pattie Belle Mosely Moody Marshall. We called her Aunt Pattie. I loved her very much and found her antics fascinating. She would repaint rather than clean house, and laid new linoleum in the kitchen almost every season. Although her eccentricities increased over the years until she had to be institutionalized with a diagnosis of manic-depression, in the summer of my eighth year she was an intriguing, animated person who I dearly loved. As I fought open the gate, I overheard Aunt Pattie coo to my mother, "The little dear has wings just like an angel." This reference to my protruding shoulder blades so

---

[2]    Micah 6:8

deflated my gate-opening triumph that I returned to the car crestfallen. Thereafter, I tended to count my ribs, notice my bony knees, and try different postures that would reduce my "angel wings."

During most of my grade school years I was bored and lonely and hungry for companionship. When I was not in school my only playmates were my younger brother and sister. At home I felt the pressure of two younger children competing for acknowledgment, and sensed growing tension between my parents. Even though I wanted to escape the farm and the crazy white folks with whom I lived, I was also intrigued by the family drama unfolding before my eyes. Reading myths and fairy tales helped me escape, and my mother was so dramatic that I became an at-home-audience-of-one for her performances.

In my mother's veins flowed the blood of poets. She was born to act. In the five-person world of our home, she was restless and irritable much of the time. However, she became effervescent and creative if we had guests or visited friends in the city. This told me she felt trapped out in the country. We both were. Mamma's solution was to escape the boredom of the farm by pursuing the life of the mind. She read Goethe aloud at breakfast, quoted Schweitzer to emphasize her points, and delivered soliloquies from Shakespeare at the slightest provocation. It was like living with Lady Macbeth. Her stories were fascinating, and although I feared her frequent unpredictable angry outbursts, I adored her and identified with her. When she decided to complete her college education by taking night classes, she became so stimulated and satisfied that I concluded education really could provide an escape from boredom.

As I approached puberty, I began spending more time with my father repairing equipment, fishing, and hunting. This opened a new world for me: a world of using my hands, trusting my body, and turning to nature. My father's family had lived over a hundred years on the same land, and Daddy had a casual intimacy with his father's five hundred eighty acres of pastures, wetlands, and woods. Exploring this Northwest Louisiana wonderland, where once the Caddo Indians had roamed, I discovered an uncanny presence and power that nourished me. Deep in the forest in the mist of dawn, a ring of mushrooms appeared where none had been the day before. High in the little limbs at the top of a beloved tree, a hawk screamed a few arm lengths away. Running through the woods high on the electric air before a thunderstorm, my feet had eyes and could find their way as surely as any wild creature. I found comfort in the spirits of the trees, and I lost myself in the magical otherworld of nature.

When the atmosphere was particularly unbearable at home, I would go to the woods about five hundred yards and another world away. I had a favorite hickory nut tree, a giant at the border between the woods and a pasture, which I would climb in stages. The beginning was difficult and required pulling myself up a complex path of gnarled stubs of broken lower branches. This part felt like I was struggling to escape the pain at home. When I finally reached the lower branches, I had an easy path up. When the trunk slimmed to a huggable human size, I would wrap myself around and melt into my beloved tree, my belly pressed against the trunk, until I felt really secure and happy. Then I made my way to the very top branches that moved with every breeze. There I could look across the fields to the forests beyond. Once when I climbed very high, I realized that our pasture separated two great forests, which created an open space of twenty acres. At this moment, I promised my tree that I would reconnect the two forests by planting trees in the pasture when I grew up. This mission grounded my love and connection to nature.

Nature also helped me find magic in myself. From an early age, I loved to hold my breath under water, and would frequently fill the bath tub to the brim and submerge for as long as possible. When I read a Boy Scout story in which the hero inhaled and exhaled deeply for several minutes before an underwater ordeal, in order to increase his lung capacity and stay under an extra minute, I immediately pulled out my watch and experimented. I was delighted to find that three minutes of deep inhales and exhales extended my ability to hold my breath from forty seconds to a minute. My breathless experiments became so vigorous that frequent floods in the bathroom motivated me to relocate to the pond, where I discovered a magical world underwater. It was completely different from underwater diving experiences in the bathtub: I could see nothing in the murky water, fish gave occasional nibbles, and I had to hold on to rocks to keep from floating. I gradually overcame the excitement of the new environment and learned to extend my time under water by relaxing and listening to the silence.

The pond

These early experiences taught me to listen. Deep in the woods, with every sense alive, I strained to hear what was out there, from the cry of an animal to the crackling twigs that would shatter the silence. When I stayed underwater in the pond, the silence that followed leaving the world "upstairs" was soon filled with the rush and roar of blood surging through my veins. As time passed, the sound of my pulse lapsed into gaps of silence, mysterious pauses. Under water I felt that the silence itself contained murmuring, rushing, almost melodic sounds. I half-believed they were fairies or water spirits. Years later I would learn that this cosmic sound behind the external sounds was "The Word" of the Bible, the *Om* that is God.[3]

---

[3] "God" is used throughout the text to indicate the Divine. It is intended in its most gender-friendly sense, no more male than female.

# *Coming of Age*

The Episcopal Church promised much, and glittered with pomp and ceremony. Each week we drove to Shreveport for Sunday services, and every few months there would be special services at All Saints, the plantation chapel my great-great-grandfather had built. When I was about fourteen, my brother, sister, and I were scheduled to have confirmation—the Episcopal version of coming of age. The services were to be conducted at All Saints by the diocese' aging, stately bishop, who was the most God-like person I could imagine. After all, several hundred people sat quietly listening to him every week, and he certainly bore a close resemblance to the conventional description of God: white hair, shining smiling face, beautiful robes, and booming voice. Preparing for the great day, I puzzled over the stained glass window my ancestors had installed at All Saints. It seemed to read, "Jam the resurrection and the life." I concluded this was a variation on the well-known Bible verse, "I am the resurrection and the life," in hopes that perhaps people in my family were surprisingly pretty cool. After all, I loved devotional hymns

All Saints

and musicians "jammed" when they played. It gave me hope that perhaps some real spiritual event would take place at the moment of confirmation.

The great day came, and so did the bishop. Representing Jesus and the spiritual aspirations of the Western world, he performed the Holiest of Holies: he gave me the body and blood of Christ. As his hand rested on my head in blessing, I hoped for a tingle, a shiver, a sign of the Holy Spirit. I watched and waited, but nothing happened. There was no juice, no electricity, no feeling. I knew much more of spirit in the top of a tree or on the porch with Aunt Emma, and I was sure that Jesus would not have settled for this charade. But nobody seemed to notice something was missing. Disappointed and confused, I numbly went through the motions and the open house celebration afterwards.

I was privileged, but I felt empty. On the "have" side, I enjoyed love and respect, and I was intelligent. My family was well connected, if not wealthy, and encouraged me to have a good education and a happy life. On the "have not" side, I felt alienated, alone, and misunderstood. I found little comfort in the knowledge that these were typical feelings for teenagers, and that pining for meaning and companionship was pretty normal.

I was also troubled by my parents' day-to day support of racial segregation, which flatly contradicted the religious and humanistic aspirations they had taught me. They seemed like hypocrites when they would not confront a racist lunatic cousin at a family gathering, and I hated them for it. The adults were all well into highballs when Cousin Hal began to rant and rave. He was a hairy bear of a man, whose career as an Air Force officer had certainly not encouraged him to develop sensitivity or listening skills. The tension grew until he proclaimed, "The world will not be a fit place until we teach the nigrahs to stay in their place and bomb the Communists back to the Stone Age."

That was too much for me, and I blurted out, "That's absolutely crazy! How can you say that?" There was complete silence for a moment. Cousin Hal grew red and seemed about to explode. Tears welled-up in my eyes, and I left the room. My mother pursued me and told me that no matter what he had been saying, I had no right to insult him and I had to apologize. She made it clear that politeness was more important than expression of true feelings or confronting outrageous political views. After a short argument and more crying, I rejoined the gathering and managed to say that, although I disagreed with his politics, I was sorry to have been rude and insulting. I was humiliated and alone, but glad Cousin Hal was not my father. If he were, he would have whipped me.

The fact that my mother was known to be somewhat unconventional relative to our family's norms probably cut me some slack in this situation. In contrast to most people in the world I knew in high school, Mamma often had very interesting points of view about issues such as war, communism, morality, or education, and saw herself as quite different from those around her. She was usually outspoken and opinionated, but did not grant me the same privilege. In our frequent confrontations, she often justified her position by using the phrase, "I cannot help it if I'm smarter than other people." Although I resented her arrogance, I continued to admire her.

As I grew into my late teens, I realized that our late night arguments were not just about mother-son differences; they had a lot to do with the fact that my father had been asleep for hours and she wanted companionship. She got stimulation during the day from her new job at Children's Protective Services of the Welfare Department, and she had more contact with friends in Shreveport, thanks to improved roads and better telephone service. However, that still did not give her companionship at home. Once inside the bounds of our home, when Mamma launched into her views about life and her dreams and plans, it was as if my father and my younger brother and sister did not exist. It seemed as if she talked only to me. I knew I had to take some distance or be overwhelmed by her neediness.

My father remained at a distance during most emotionally charged situations. When the stress level increased, he left the house to do farm chores, and my mother became convinced that he drank whiskey at the barn before returning. I was torn between loving and hating him. I was deeply ashamed of his apparent weakness, and felt that the name "Henry" meant "inadequate." To preserve some respect for him and my own self-esteem (after all we shared the same name), I cherished his flashes of assertiveness in the rare moments when he showed his anger. As our baseball coach, he stopped a ball game and confronted the bullying coach of the opposing team. When a wild dog attacked my brother out in the pasture, Daddy chased the animal away and threw a hammer a huge distance, hitting him on the run. Once when my mother went ballistic in the kitchen, my father yelled at her and threw a skillet on the floor, while we three children cheered. The quiet strength of my father was revealed to me much more often when he guided the work of black men in our fields and dairy. He was considerate and respectful, and handled inadequacies and mistakes in a way that made clear what needed fixing, while allowing the person at fault to save face. My father was master of his farm world, and diligently persevered under terrible economic conditions that put many other farms out of business. He was, however, so incapable of talking about emotional issues that I felt little support and virtually no guidance when I was upset and reached out to him.

I particularly missed my father's guidance about sex. In its absence, well-intended and rather academic communications from my mother gave the strong impression that the intensity of my erupting sexuality was dangerous. I felt that I was abnormal when I got erections in school, or fantasized and masturbated at night. Outwardly my parents' message was simple and adamant: "Do not get a girl pregnant or you will ruin your life!" In visions that defied logic and gravity, I imagined that my future might hinge on one determined, hyperactive sperm that could swim through clothes and condoms, and hike up a warm leg to impregnate an alluring ovum. A little petting and a lot of masturbation seemed like my best option. To both of my parents, the former was barely acceptable, and the latter was definitely not. My feelings of loneliness and guilt grew.

I had fun with my teenage friends, but it was almost exclusively conditional upon being cool or smart, being an athlete or having a car. We could enjoy soul music and be open to black culture, but I could not trust them to understand or accept my mystical connection to nature, so I did not tell them. My mistrust came from being the butt of one-too-many jokes, like the time two buddies and our basketball coach almost choked to death with laughter as I walked across an opposing team's gymnasium to meet them. I was sporting a new haircut that provoked the joke, "Marshall is so skinny, with that haircut he looks like a walking lollipop." I completed high school outwardly successful and honored, but inwardly aching to be accepted.

High school basketball player

# *Longing for the Light*

I went to college confident that I would get a good education, and optimistic that I would have sexual and spiritual experiences, and find an enlightening teacher I could emulate. By the spring of my first year away from home at the University of the South, in Sewanee, Tennessee, I began to develop new close friendships. This was a delight and a relief. Moreover, the luscious landscape of the Cumberland Plateau in the foothills of the Smoky Mountains made me ecstatic, and I was interested in much of what I was studying. However, I was critical, judgmental, and self-righteous when confronted with professors, heads of departments, and university administrators who offered themselves as role models, while flaunting their various addictions to nicotine, alcohol, and self-aggrandizement. I recognized them as brilliant academicians, but was put off by their arrogance. I also distrusted my classmates who groveled before them. The few teachers I loved were not posturing as great because they had international reputations in their fields. They were great because they could guide me into the enchanted world of their special knowledge. My new friends quenched my thirst for acceptance, and my mentors ignited my imagination.

In my first spring away from home, revolution was in the air. The Vietnam War was grinding its way toward my draft number, Martin Luther King and hundreds of thousands of people had a dream, and psychedelics promised to open new levels of consciousness for the courageous and the curious. Fascinated by the prospects of expanding my consciousness, and having begun trying marijuana at Christmas time, by Easter I was ready to graduate to LSD. This was very soberly undertaken as a way to explore altered states of awareness. I studied *The Psychedelic Experience:* a manual for consciousness exploration, based on Tibetan teachings about after-death states, written by Timothy Leary, Ralph Metzner, and Richard Alpert. My first psychedelic experience brought thrilling glimpses of clear light beaming through fast-moving clouds. I wanted to experience more of this white light. I understood that drugs were merely a chemical key to transcendent states, and began looking for a guide who knew transcendent states from the inside, who lived them in daily life, and who could teach me to do the same.

At about that time, my newfound college friend, who practiced yoga and meditation, let me borrow his copy of Paramahansa Yogananda's *Autobiography of a Yogi*. Something woke up in me and said, "Ah Ha!" when I discovered the fundamental tenet of mysticism: individuals can have direct communion or union with God. After this realization, other new ideas seemed obvious to me. For instance, that a Divine Mother is just as suitable a focus of devotion as is God the Father; or that Jesus was not the only divine incarnation to walk the Earth or the only enlightened being to assist the spiritual evolution of humanity.

I found the concept of *karma*[4] provided a frame for understanding and taking distance from the circumstances of my life, from the blessings and the burdens, from the privileges and the pain. In Yogananda's autobiography I heard echoes of the struggle I had with my family, and his triumphant spiritual life gave me hope. With new understanding gleaned from his book, I realized my parents were saying, "You cannot escape your responsibility to us and to what we have given you. Only by fulfilling your worldly responsibilities can you live a godly life." Some inner part of me was struggling to say, "Any heavy responsibility, any problem, any karma can be overcome by focusing on God."

Reading Yogananda's story gave me the feeling for the first time in my life that my life could be really happy. I really knew who I was, and that I had a place in the scheme of things. I realized I was just like everyone else. The human condition is to struggle with the circumstance of life, to be blessed and burdened by karma, and to seek to fulfill one's destiny. This realization pointed beyond my immediate goal of getting educated to escape the farm and Southern closed-mindedness. I saw that I needed to learn to meditate in order to recognize the limitations of my background, and to learn to live consciously in order to work out these limitations in the course of life. Taking Yogananda as a role model meant being initiated by a master into the highest teachings I could assimilate, and eventually spreading that wisdom to the

---

[4]  The effects of past actions, in this or a former life; from Sanskrit "kri" (to do).

best of my ability. It sounded like a great life plan to a teenage boy who was finally starting to feel at home in the universe.

# II. Guidance

> *The basic tool of evolution is metamorphosis. If a "lil ol fuzzie" caterpillar can molt four times and then become a butterfly, well sir, I think that's the least we can do. Mutation is the scary concept. Each species dreads the future. Darwin is a horror when people realize that evolution is continuing. This is the idea which has amused and cheered me the most. We are embryonic creatures. Not even born yet.*
>
> Timothy Leary (1975)

## Meeting a Remarkable Man

I was thrilled at the idea of using ancient wisdom to help our troubled world—and myself. I enrolled in the Self-Realization Fellowship (SRF) Lessons (Yogananda, 1956), a study course designed to prepare students for initiation[5] into Kriya Yoga, a technique Yogananda had brought from India to the West, as a means for Westerners to reach the heights of spiritual attainment. The SRF Lessons presented a program of study and practice of yogic disciplines that prepared students for initiation over a

---

[5] Refers to ceremonial acknowledgement by a teacher or guru that a student or disciple has reached a certain level of proficiency, and has earned the right to join an inner circle. It also refers to instruction given during the initiation ceremony.

two-year period. With infinity calling, this may not sound like much time, but I was impatient. I was still thirsty for the "juice" I never got at my first communion. I wanted initiation from a living master, and was not very motivated by the idea of a ceremony at the end of a correspondence course, even if the lessons were about self-realization.

I knew somewhere in this world I could find my own *guru*[6] to help me learn to meditate and become aware enough to serve others, promote justice, and reveal truth. From reading Yogananda's autobiography, I became fixed on the idea of meeting a master. The term "master" was frequently used in Yogananda's book to refer to one's own beloved guru, as well as to refer to anyone who had mastered the higher yogic states of *samadhi*.[7] Yogananda wrote that the specific super-conscious states that give proof that someone is a master are the ability to enter the breathless state at will and the attainment of immutable bliss. To rein in my intense fascination with attaining these transcendent states, I focused instead on the (hopefully) more immediate goal of mastering the illusions and delusions of the ego. I felt that initiation meant entering a deep relationship of commitment and trust with someone who had achieved this mastery, and who could help me achieve it as well.

Linus Sharp, the friend who had loaned me *Autobiography of a Yogi*, offered to take me to his home in Houston during the summer break to introduce me to Adano Ley, an initiate of Yogananda whom Linus considered a master. The first evening we were in Houston, Linus drove us from his parents' suburban home to a *sat sang*[8] that Adano would conduct. As we left the freeways, the daytime heat of June began to ease, and twilight crept through the tree-lined neighborhood of Montrose, the area of the city with the greatest concentration of longhairs, students, and artists. We approached a small church where about thirty people were milling around and seating themselves on the lawn. Someone said it was just too hot inside, so we were

---

[6] Spiritual teacher, dispeller of darkness; from Sanskrit "gu" (darkness), and "ru" (that which dispels).

[7] Blissful superconscious state in which the breath slows to a stop, and the individual soul and Cosmic Spirit are perceived as identical.

[8] From Sanskrit "sat" (truth), and "sang" (fellowship).

going to be outside. Then I saw Adano, an ageless man with a compact body, Asian features, shining black hair, and radiant eyes. I felt immediately drawn to him and I enjoyed his talk, especially his frequent references to physics and biology in order to explain meditation. After talking for about an hour, he answered questions. Sometimes he was very direct, even confrontive, as if he knew the person was deeply involved with the issue in question. At other times he responded with a joke, as if to say, "You're looking in the wrong direction with that question." Sometimes a simple question led to a deep, extended discourse. After about another hour, he guided the group into a meditation that lasted about twenty minutes. I was pretty focused, even when an occasional mosquito flew by my ear. I felt a wave of peace flow through me followed by a sense of deep joy. My skin tingled and prickled, and I felt a shiver totally out of place in the velvety warmth of the evening air. These sensations were evidence that something wonderful was happening. This was the kind of experience I had sought at my first communion. I was confident that Adano could initiate me and start me on my way.

Adano worked in an engineering job inspecting pipes and was married to a chiropractor. What a relief to see this wonderful man going about his business in the chaos of Houston, rather than to imagine that great yogis only lived in the Himalayas. As much as I yearned for enlightenment, I did not want to have to renounce the world and become a monk. I had read in Yogananda's writings that great yogis might be found in any walk of life, but until I met Adano, I had never seen one. Like Yogananda, Adano taught that it was important to faithfully fulfill family, business, civic, and spiritual responsibilities without personal motive or attachment.

Although I was relieved to find a role model of a "householder" yogi in Adano, I still understood yogic teachings from the point of view of an adolescent overwhelmed with sexual desires and conditioned by parents and society to repress them for fear of fathering an unwanted baby. I felt that, like a monk, I should conserve my sexual energy and that I should be following advice given to Yogananda by his guru, Sri Yukteswar. "Daily renewed sense yearnings sap your inner peace; they are like openings in a reservoir that permit vital waters to be wasted in the desert soil of materialism. The forceful, activating impulse of wrong desire is the greatest enemy to the happiness of man. Roam in the world as a lion of self-control; do not let the frogs of sense weakness kick you around!" Since I gave at least as much time and energy to solo sexual practice as I did to spiritual practice, I felt more a frog than a lion.

Driven by rampaging sexuality and frustrated at attempts to meditate and practice yoga, I became increasingly self-critical over the following months. If I were too heterosexually driven to become a monk, how would I develop a love relationship at a college attended only by men? How could I continue a spiritual path so distracted by sexual impulses? My college was hundreds of miles from that of my high school sweetheart, Susan Strean. We were rapidly approaching a point where we either needed to get closer or we would drift apart. I felt more loving respect than passion for her, and hoped that my conservative upbringing, supported by metaphysical

Young bridegroom and parents

longings, could somehow control my horny hormones. At Christmas we made a decision: we would marry in June and move to Houston to continue college at a new school where I could pursue my spiritual path with Adano's help.

Married life with Susan was not as big a change for me as was moving to an urban metropolis. After a few nights in Houston, I realized I had never spent that much time in a city. The noise of traffic filtered into our garage apartment above the whoosh of the perpetually running air conditioner. Susan and I clung to each other, two people isolated in the midst of a huge impersonal city. We were barely twenty years old during the turbulent last years of the sixties. We insulated ourselves from the world by playing house, and studied and worked our way through the University of Houston. The main tension between us was my intense desire to spend time with Adano. Though I did not really value private time with Susan, I did recognize that it was her right to want it. I juggled my schedule trying to keep the stress low in our relationship, and only attended sat sang on occasion.

The tremendous advantage of direct contact with Adano as a spiritual teacher, rather than relying exclusively on books and my SRF Lessons, was that he relieved my guilt at not being the ideal yogi I dreamed of becoming. This so encouraged me that I dreamed of receiving initiation right away because I was so sincere. But Adano only gave initiations when the time was right, and I had to relax and trust that some-day the time would be right for me. As Adano put it, "You are at the right place at the right time for the right experience."[9] The right time and place for initiation took a lot more time than I imagined.

---

[9]  In *Diamond Body* (1996), and in *Butterflies Need No Taxidermist* (1997), Ed Bergstrom has published numerous quotes from Adano, along with extensive commentary. Where I have not been able to remember Adano's exact words, I have relied on these sources.

# *Initiating the Quest*

Once when I nudged Adano a little too hard about wanting to get initiated, he fixed me with a dark glance and said, "Understanding is coping. Non-understanding is looking for a shortcut." Taken aback, I realized that my vision of myself as a yogi was of a sixty year old who lived in the Himalayas, and I was a twenty year old living in Houston. There was no shortcut. I had to be here now. As soon as I accepted this, I felt less stress. I realized that as much as I wanted to live near Adano, I would be much happier out of the city. Susan and I decided to complete our undergraduate studies at Sewanee, which had just announced that it would begin admitting female students. Within a month of our move to Sewanee, Adano gave a sat sang nearby, and Susan agreed to join the group that evening. To my utter amazement, Adano offered initiation that evening, and Susan and I were initiated together. The fact that Adano chose to initiate Susan made me value her spirituality, and my giving her this acknowledgment made our relationship more peaceful.

As a result of initiation, I also began to understand the importance of the breath and mantras for experiencing higher levels of consciousness. Adano taught that, "The whole body is timed internally according to the lungs. Breathing determines levels of consciousness, but you have to be awake! Lungs take precedence over the brain …. Mantra functions to slow down the brain to the rate of the heart, thereby giving us the ability to see into the electrical field, rather than to simply look at the outer form …. Place the conviction in the sonics; do not put your faith in the optics. You fixate to an optic; you merge with the sonics." As I worked to unravel this involved teaching, I began to recognize that a lot of my attraction to spiritual development had come from my fascination with idealized images, i.e., optics. I was fascinated with imitating Jesus and of being an ideal yogi. I also hoped to see shining angels and radiant beings. I realized that to "place conviction in sonics," I needed to listen and to chant mantras.

Yogananda's autobiography had introduced me to mantras as sacred chants in Sanskrit language that have transformative power over all natural phenomena. The potencies of sound and of the human voice have been extensively studied in India for thousands of years. There it is taught that all sounds have powers derived from *Om*[10], the "hum of the Cosmic Motor," which brings into manifestation the qualities of creation, preservation, and destruction. The psychological and mathematical perfection of Sanskrit, the world's most ancient language, together with discoveries of artifacts from an extremely ancient and highly developed culture in India, suggest that mantras are remnants of a wisdom we can only dimly imagine. Mantras are a sophisticated development of this culture which, when correctly pronounced, have what Yogananda called, "a spiritually beneficial vibratory potency."

For the next eighteen months, I faithfully practiced the mantra and meditation methods Adano gave in initiation. I focused on silently chanting a mantra to quiet the breath so I could hear the audible life stream (the Om). Once the novelty of the new mantra and new information wore off, my efforts at meditation were a struggle to concentrate and to keep my mind from wandering or falling asleep. Although from time to time an experience would thrill me, often I was very bored doing the same spiritual practice day after day. I told myself that this was just my resistance to change, but it did not help very much.

Yogananda and Adano both taught other methods that I began to use with more success. Preparing for meditation by first taking a shower and putting on clean, loose-fitting clothes helped me feel alert, relaxed, and ready for something special. Reserving a little space in our apartment for spiritual practices also helped me feel the "specialness" of what was happening, and guided my imagination in the direction of devotion, so I made a little altar in part of a spare room. I filled this room with candles, flowers, and pictures of my spiritual role models: Yogananda and his gurus, along with Jesus and Adano. I felt that these positive visual images helped counterbalance the violent imagery that bombarded me through media. Before beginning to chant or meditate it helped to stretch and energize my body. I practiced techniques from Yogananda's SRF Lessons, did a little yoga, and breathed deep. All in all, between showering, stretching, and preparing the room, it took at least thirty min-

---

[10]   Also written AUM; the primordial vibratory power behind all atomic energies.

utes to get ready to chant mantras and meditate. I then did my best to spend at least an hour (sometimes as much as two hours) of focused sadhana, or spiritual practice.

Given the amount of time I spent on spiritual practices each day, along with my self-righteous, holier-than-thou attitude, it is amazing that I did not drive Susan completely crazy. I had tremendous emotional energy tied up in the tension I created between my spiritual aspirations versus life in the world. I struggled with the question: "How can I pursue my quest for consciousness and get an education that leads to a profession working with people?" When we graduated from Sewanee, Susan and I knew we would go on to graduate school. Her area was mathematics, and I planned to study religion. However, while visiting my parents, my plans changed. My mother was becoming paranoid. She was convinced that the Louisiana Department of Education was sending airplanes, helicopters, and automobiles to make loud noise and drive her crazy because she had criticized some of their policies when she had served on the school board. At times she became very irrational and would run out of the house yelling at passing cars. My father maintained a reserved, genteel distance from my mother's deterioration, and took refuge in increasing amounts of whiskey. This shocked and disturbed me, and brought me off my spiritual pedestal into the world of family and responsibility. During my unsuccessful struggle to get my mother to see a doctor and my father to face what was happening to her, I learned more and more about psychopathology. I began to think that by studying clinical psychology I might learn something that would help my parents, while providing me with a satisfying career.

My spiritual life ebbed and flowed over the next eight years as I made my way through graduate school in clinical psychology at the University of Tennessee, and an internship and post-doctoral studies back in Houston. Even though my minor in religious studies gave some academic credibility to my "otherworldly" interests, there was little place for spirituality in clinical psychology at the University of Tennessee. I detected disinterest and skepticism among professors in the humanistic track I followed, and it was better not to mention the subject at all to the behavioral or psychodynamic people. Nobody in our program would sponsor Adano to speak to my clinical classmates because meditation and yoga were simply too far out.

I was determined to bring Adano into at least the periphery of my studies, and arranged for him to speak at the student union, rather than at the psychological clinic. I learned I could successfully pursue my interests without support from my mentors. However, I was disappointed that not one of my fellow clinical students attended Adano's talk.

This motivated me to begin working hard to build a place for spirituality in my life as a clinical psychologist by writing a dissertation on Timothy Leary's work in consciousness expansion. My professors were wonderfully supportive of my investigation of this notorious psychologist, who was for me a role model. After having my first psychedelic experiences in college with the guidance of Leary's writings, I rediscovered him in graduate school in the mid-1970s as the author of a required text. His early work in *Interpersonal Diagnosis of Personality* (1957) gave such clear insight into psychological functioning that I began to look deeper into his life and work, only to find that he was in prison. His advocacy of consciousness expansion and criticism of authority had become so influential in the late 1960s that Richard Nixon had labeled him "the most dangerous man in America." Thereafter he was imprisoned for possession of a marijuana cigarette. To me this seemed like persecuting Socrates for corrupting the youth of Athens.

Leary responded to my study of his life by telephoning me from prison and writing a detailed letter of positive feedback. Our relationship developed over the next several years when he was released from prison, and was an important influence as I began the transition from student to professional. His message to me was to stay skeptical of all social systems (professional psychology, the institution of marriage, universities, the church, etc.), and rely on scientific method rather than religious belief to understand consciousness.

As I entered the profession of psychology, I felt like a well-trained renegade. I had earned the right to join the elite club of Clinical Psychologists, but I did not feel like I belonged. I felt that my intention to use my psychological training and credentials to boldly explore human potential was not shared by many of my colleagues, and could easily be perceived by them as threatening.

Despite my skepticism of professional psychology, I began teaching and started a clinical practice. I also cautiously introduced yogic breathing techniques to my students and clients. They learned to reduce stress by breathing slowly and deeply, letting their bellies and then their chests fill up with air, and being conscious not to catch or stop the breath at any point in the cycle of inhaling and exhaling. I really enjoyed teaching psychology at Texas Southern University (TSU)—which was originally called *The University of Negroes* when it opened in 1950. There I supervised minority students in clinical programs, and helped them gain access to placements in the Texas Medical Center where I had trained, but where TSU's other faculty had few contacts. I felt very satisfied using my newly achieved power and position to give opportunities to black students. Somehow, I felt I was also paying a debt of gratitude to Aunt Emma, and making up for my family's racist heritage. There was so much to do personally and in the world of psychology that I only meditated when I really needed to. I began to accept myself as I was in the present—a sexy, skinny seeker—and stopped looking ahead to somehow becoming a saint.

As rewarding as these developments were inwardly and professionally, nothing I learned or did as a psychologist really helped my mother or my father. My mother did not want to be helped to become less paranoid. She just wanted to feel safe and loved. When my younger brother and sister moved out of the house to go to college, she insisted that my father control his drinking, and he did. Then they began to enjoy each other more, and her paranoia mellowed somewhat.

My training also did not help Susan and me find happiness together. Even though we shared interests and aspirations, I felt trapped in domestic bondage and, as in the past, was starved for passion and intimacy. In graduate school we drew closer after I had individual therapy and we attended a few sessions of marriage counselling. However, after leaving the close-knit community that university life provided us, our differences widened and became more painful until we drifted inexorably apart. As is so often the case, our first baby came and drew us together, so we planned for a second baby in hopes of rekindling our relationship. As Susan was about to give birth, I felt like I was about to suffocate and die. At this worst of all imaginable times I realized I had to leave Susan as a marriage partner, and yet somehow maintain a supportive, respectful friendship with her as the mother of our children.

42

# *Cleaning the Stable*

One spring evening in 1979, in the midst of divorce, I desperately needed to talk with Adano. I found that he had a new address, and easily made my way to the apartment complex where he lived. But then I searched almost an hour without being able to find his home. I got disoriented going through a huge parking garage, and began to feel that my search for Adano was symbolic of the ordeal I was experiencing in my life. It seemed as if I somehow was not being allowed to find Adano when I was desperate for his advice. Instead, I had to trust myself. With these ideas pounding in my brain, I finally stumbled into his apartment. I became calm almost the instant I entered the door. Then I was amazed to hear that Adano was getting a divorce, too. He had married within a few months of Susan and me, and now he was leaving his ten-year marriage. This synchronicity helped me feel less alone and eased the intense guilt I felt at leaving Susan and the boys.

After that, it took about two years of intense sexual experimentation and professional role exploration before I realized that what I really wanted was a steady job helping people as a psychologist, an apartment convenient for having the boys on weekends, and participation in a spiritual community. I got a job with the Houston public schools, helping emotionally disturbed students, and rented an apartment in Adano's complex. I wanted my sons to get the feel of a spiritual community in their early years, a little like I had with the black families on our farm. Adam, a five-year-old sage, and David, a two-year-old showman, fit right in at Adano's place. The atmosphere was like a meditative Chinese restaurant stuffed with items from a garage sale. Over the next two years, my daily exposure to the remarkable wisdom of this enigmatic shaman helped me begin to take responsibility for my own health through reflexology, colonics, and solar nutrition.

Adano advocated and practiced a comprehensive approach to what he called "longevity life-styles": heal disorders by detoxifying the body, maintain health through good nutrition, and evolve spiritually using subtle techniques like Kriya yoga and chanting mantras. For detoxifying, Adano first deeply massaged the nerve points in the feet to get the body's energy flowing and stimulate internal organs to release toxins. This reflexology treatment was typically followed by irrigating the colon with a sustained gentle flow of water through a speculum inserted in the rectum.

Adano had his colonic room arranged so that you could see the waste flowing out a clear plastic tube. The colonic treatment released amazing things from your bowels that you knew you had not eaten in years. It was a little like finding a car battery in a shark's belly. Sounds bizarre—worked wonders. Then followed the question: "What do you do after you clean out the crap?"

Adano prepared and served a delicious lunch and dinner according to a system

Adano with a solar nutrition diagram

called solar nutrition. It advocates eating foods at the time of day when that food was most activated by the sun. Morning foods grow on trees and get the first sunlight: many fruits, nuts, etc. Mid-day foods grow on the ground up to four feet high and get direct sun from noon to late afternoon: grains, many vegetables, berries, etc. Night foods grow in darkness underground or right at the surface of the ground: potatoes, pineapples, peanuts, etc. It is a fun system that allows you to eat almost anything, if it is at the right time of day. There was even a period three days before and three days after the full moon, for eating any combination without problems. Adano called this lunar nutrition (also lunar madness). It is nice to have a diet that lets you cheat. The theory is that by eating the right foods at the right time of day, the body is best able to use them and we continue to detoxify and nourish ourselves. Solar nutrition added a way to be healthy and well-fed to my more-or-less vegetarian diet. Besides, I was a bachelor, and I liked Adano's cooking.

With this basis of detoxification and nutrition, more subtle methods like meditation and mantra chanting can then facilitate evolution effectively.[11] Adano considered using these subtle methods without the basics to be misplaced effort. For detoxification, Adano calculated that, "One hour of bodywork (such as reflexology) is worth three hours of meditation. One colonic is worth a thousand hours of meditation." Eliminating an average person's extreme toxicity with the more subtle methods is like cleaning a stable with a toothbrush: better use a shovel. He scoffed at people who equated sensational meditation experiences with progress. "Do not con-

---

[11] Specific mantras and techniques conveyed in initiation cannot be taught in this book, because they require initiation to be practiced correctly. However, it is important to understand that all practice of yogic breathing and mantra chanting is designed to reap the benefits of quieting the breath. As the breath quiets, the brain rhythms slow, and the body relaxes. Conversely, when we are activated, tensed, or stressed, the breath is fast and irregular, and the brain generates fast-wave activity at about forty to forty-five cycles per second (cps). As we relax and the breath slows, we enter alpha brain rhythms at eight to twelve cps, associated with a pleasant experience of peacefulness. As breath slows even more, meditation deepens and rhythmical theta waves appear at six to seven cps. It is only upon entering delta brain rhythms of one to two cps, the brain activity associated with deep sleep and very deep meditation, that we experience a naturally occurring pause between the exhale and the inhale, a timeless space that some call *nirvana*.

fuse illness with attainment," he said, explaining that most of the phenomena people experience in meditation—from physical jerking and shaking to psychic communications—have more to do with the release of toxins than with spiritual attainment. Toxin releases are a healthy step, but should be undertaken with the appropriate methods, and not be confused with meditative awareness: they are static, not the signal.

By combining solar nutrition, bodywork, and colonics, I became healthier and life was less chaotic. As I practiced these detoxification methods, I noticed that the yogic breathing techniques and mantras I had struggled with for over a decade began to take me deeper into meditation.

When I became intoxicated with intense inner experiences that made the daily world seem like a shadow, Adano helped me come back to earth. With his own special combination of humor and mental gymnastics, he acknowledged my experiences and put them in a larger context. After a meditation in which I shivered and my skin tingled with goose bumps, Adano said, "God comes as cold chills." Then he added, "Mantras are breathless delta brainwave programming. They trigger environmental biophysics. A meditator tunes in on the 'vibes.' The vibes are goose bumps, biological stimulation of the pores. God is pure physics."

Adano often said that meditation actually is "Mental energy directing individual thought activities toward intuitive observation and oneness with noumenon." The Greek word *noumenon* is a synonym for reality, for the ground of phenomena that is unknowable by the senses. After ten years of practice, I began to follow the breath into this timeless dimension of heightened experiences of reality. I felt as if I was finally reaping a rich harvest from the struggles and initiations of years before.

# III. Discovery

*We read in the Bhagavatam[12] that the Lord has declared, "Kali Yuga[13] is full of evil propensities, but there is one great characteristic which it has, and that is that just by chanting the Holy Name one attains mukti[14]." Is it not as simple as that? People want to make it very difficult. God says, "I am very easily attainable in Kali Yuga," but we want to make it very difficult. You can make God as easy or as difficult as you want. Convert yourself to an innocent babe, call His Name, and He will appear.*

Sant Keshavadas (1979)

## Sing the Holy Name

One afternoon in the spring of 1981, Adano suggested I come over that evening. I still recall my excitement at his invitation because his personal invitations were so rare. Things just happened around Adano. I arrived on time, and when I entered the room I found about twenty-five people sitting cross-legged on the floor. A few min-

---

[12]  One of the sacred texts of Hinduism.

[13]  Age of materialism in Hindu cosmology.

[14]  Joy of liberation.

utes later a shining brown man entered the room, surrounded by a wave of golden light. I joined my palms at my heart and bowed my head, as did most of the group. It seemed totally natural when confronted with such a remarkable presence. As the resonant voice of Satguru Sant Keshavadas[15] filled the room, my neck hair stood on end. I lifted my head and gazed at him in wonder. It felt as if a bolt of light entered into me. For the rest of the evening I was filled with a buzzing, bubbling sensation, as he told stories, sang songs, and chanted mantras from the Himalayas. This radiant Indian guru overflowed with loving wisdom and awakened feelings I had not known since being enchanted by the fairies and cradled by the trees back at the farm.

I burned with excitement, yet felt an indescribable peace. In daily life I may have been a clinical psychologist caring for many disturbed students, but I stumbled up to Keshavadas at the end of the evening like a three-year-old approaching Santa Claus. Somehow I knew he was my guru, my own special link to the Divine. Much later I learned that the holy scriptures of the East teach that if on meeting a person without introduction, even for a moment, you feel a peace which you have never enjoyed before, and if your hair stands on end, and your palms join with head bent, the one you are meeting should be considered your guru (Keshavadas, 1976b). This evening I just knew it through intuition.

When I told Keshavadas about the light that had come into me, he smiled sweetly and said, "You are very blessed. Panduranga[16] has entered into you. Come with me to India." In a few months Sant Keshavadas would be making his XVI Global Tour, which would culminate in a World Peace Conference in India. Devotees were invited to accompany him on a pilgrimage to the Himalayas and other sacred centers in India. I was overwhelmed at the idea. Meeting my guru and going to India; it was happening so fast!

Because I was barely pulling out of a financial crisis following divorce and was unable to afford the pilgrimage, Keshavadas gave me a mantra for noble wealth. He

---

[15]  *Satguru* means "True Guru," true dispeller of darkness. *Sant Keshavadas* means "Saint who is the servant of the Lord."

[16]  Incarnation of Vishnu, the preserver, active in this era in human history; God as the White Light.

instructed me to chant *Om Srim Mahalakshmyai* one hundred eight times each day for forty days with sincere devotion, and I would have enough money for the pilgrimage (Keshavadas, 1980). I felt his absolute sincerity and said I would do it. However, I had many questions. Some I managed to ask right away; others came to me later. Keshavadas answered many questions over the next few days as I accompanied him when he conducted *sat sang* and *puja*[17] around Houston.

For the fullest benefits, Keshavadas said to chant mantras with devotion (*Bhakti*), and action in the form of either external or internal worship (*Kriya*). I was so excited by the feelings of love I felt in Keshavadas' presence that I realized I could now experience far more intense devotion than ever before. Although I had often performed worshipful actions in connection with meditating (such as lighting candles), I began to realize that compared to the fervor I felt at Keshavadas' pujas, my normal observances were frequently half-conscious and ritualistic, rather than awake and meaningful. At his ceremonies, lighting candles and incense (external actions) and visualizing throwing my faults into a ceremonial fire (internal action) noticeably mobilized positive energy. Psychologically these worshipful actions acknowledge allegiance to a higher purpose, not to simple ego gratification. These new ways of understanding helped me stop worrying about my problems with money and my desire for more. I threw myself into chanting the mantra wholeheartedly.

When chanting a mantra one hundred eight times, Keshavadas advised the following. The first thirty-six repetitions are uttered with full voice, paying attention to the right intonation, pronunciation, and pauses. The second thirty-six repetitions are muttered with a very low voice, moving only the lips and tongue, while paying attention to the meaning of the mantra. The last thirty-six repetitions are in the mind, with attention absorbed in the meaning, feeling and hearing the mantra in the heart. Finally, one enters into perfect silence, allowing the tongue to rest against the roof of the mouth.

When I questioned the significance of chanting a mantra one hundred eight uninterrupted repetitions each day for forty consecutive days, I found that the Himalayan

---

[17]    Ritual worship ceremony.

tradition describes a metaphysical nervous system in which one hundred eight energy channels—*nadis*—go through the heart center. I knew from Adano that every forty days the physical body replaces its mineral constituents, thereby becoming effectively a "new" body. Therefore, I reasoned that the repetition of a mantra for one hundred eight times a day for forty days fills the heart each day, and locks the vibration into the body for a full "mineral cycle." This literally fills your body with the mantra's vibration, thereby stabilizing the positive effects of the mantra in you. Keshavadas confirmed this understanding of the teaching, adding that although one hundred eight times a day is usually a recommended minimum there is no absolute rule about this.

I was not clear how to go about the actual technique of counting one hundred eight mantra repetitions while maintaining devoted concentration, and once again received detailed instruction from Keshavadas. Simply counting on the fingers with the tip of the thumb is sufficient for counting mantra repetitions—which are called *japa*. Or the counting can be done with a string of beads called a *mala*—similar to the rosary in the West.

Malas are often made from the seed of a holy tree (rudrakshi or sandalwood, for example), and are sometimes made of crystals, jewels, or conch shells, all of which have various abilities to hold the vibration of the mantra. The number of beads on a mala are either one hundred eight plus one, or fifty-four plus one. The single bead hangs separate from the rest and is called the *meru*. It symbolizes the axis of the universe and the spinal column. The beads are held between the thumb tip and middle joint of the middle finger of the right hand. To count one hundred eight repetitions, start with the mala held so that the meru is away from the body. Make one repetition of the mantra with the thumb and middle finger on the first bead; push it away from the body to go to the second bead for the second repetition; continue until you come to the meru. In the case of a fifty-four-bead mala, reverse directions when you reach the meru after repetition fifty-four, and begin drawing the beads toward the body. Whatever number of repetitions you choose, do not cross the meru—use it as a reference point.

Any other method to count repetitions is fine, if it gets the job done. The most high-tech method is to make a cassette copy of a mantra, and end the recording after one hundred eight repetitions. You just chant along with the support of the recording and go into silence when it ends. I found it extremely helpful to record Keshavadas' resonate intonations in order to feel the mantra's vibration for a number of repetitions, then I would go on chanting using a mala for the rest of the count.

Although one hundred eight repetitions is a recommended minimum in monastic life, where devotees chant ten times or even a hundred times this much in a day, one hundred eight repetitions stretched my devotional and meditative capacities when I did it daily. The mantra Keshavadas gave me could be chanted in about five seconds, so I blazed through one hundred eight in about ten minutes.

The hard thing for me was to concentrate and stay devotional throughout. Varying the breath helped a lot. I knew that although breath regulates the body and controls consciousness, it is not the focus of devotional chanting. The obvious path seemed to be to remember to take full breaths while chanting out loud, and focus on the mantra. I settled on a method of beginning the mantra repetitions with my eyes open and focusing on a candle, a flower, or an image of a deity. Then as I progressed in the repetitions, I would let my eyes close and focus my attention at the middle of my forehead. I got into the practice, the more energy I gave the mantra repetitions, the more focused I stayed. If the devotional practice led to chanting silently and the breath slowed and even paused or stopped, a door opened into expanded consciousness. If not, I knew I had done my best and that I would give it a go the next day.

As the end of Keshavadas' visit to Houston neared, I stocked up on copies of his books and recordings, and readied myself for the upcoming period when he would be far away. As I said good-bye to him at the airport, I emotionally confessed that I felt he was my guru, and that I would do my best to follow his teachings. He placed his hand on my head and blessed me with Sanskrit words I did not understand. However, I felt such peace and joy that there was nothing more I could wish. As a grown man with two children, kneeling in the boarding area of Houston Intercontinental Airport before an Indian guru clad in yellow silk robes, I finally felt the peace and direct contact to the Divine that I had yearned for since childhood. If the bishop could see me now!

# *Cowboys and Indians*

I chanted the mantra each morning before going to work. I imagined I was chanting to the Divine Goddess Mother whose benevolent generosity sustains all life. From the beginning I somehow knew that a path would open that would let me go on the pilgrimage to India. In my job as a school psychologist for Houston Independent School District, I had responsibilities at forty schools that stretched across the sprawling city. That meant I drove a lot. As soon as I got in my car I would start one of Keshavadas' tapes and chant along with him, singing at the top of my lungs until I reached my destination. In Keshavadas' voice I heard a Divine Presence. Absorbed in the experience, and driving at the same time, the intricacies of Indian music were all but lost on me. I chanted the text with the melody on the refrains, and chanted the ground tone or a simple harmony when Keshavadas soared into virtuosity. Later in the day, passages from the recordings would flow into my mind and I would chant to myself, sometimes with a text Keshavadas had sung, and sometimes with the mantra he had given me. Nearing the end of the forty days I received a letter from an oil and gas business offering to buy mineral rights on part of my family land in Louisiana. It was just enough to let me pay my debts and go on the pilgrimage. To me it felt like a miracle!

I was elated for weeks and made preparations for the trip. Keshavadas gave me the mantra *Om Sri Ram Jai Ram Jai Jai Ram* to prepare for the peace pilgrimage. Buzzing with an ecstatic frenzy, I chanted it almost constantly. When I got a little bored I changed melodies to renew my interest. Even hearing pop songs played in a shop could not distract me from the mantra. I simply chanted the mantra with the pop song melody. Improvising and integrating Western music with mantra chanting seemed a natural way to fulfill my intention to quiet my internal chatter, shield myself from the noise pollution of daily life, and stay high with devotion.

As the departure for India loomed before me, I suddenly began to question what I was doing. I wondered, "If Keshavadas is my guru, who is Adano to me?" Adano said it was like in the army: the guru is like the sergeant in boot camp who teaches recruits to avoid killing themselves with their own weapon; the satguru is like the general who takes recruits after they are trained, and tells them their mission. This bizarre metaphor was so on target! From Adano I had learned and was still learning how to detoxify and to meditate. From Keshavadas I was going to learn something else, but I did not know what. Adano's irreverent humor had once again jolted me out of my worries, and prepared me for my adventure.

The pilgrimage proceeded through South India, then north to Katmandu, Nepal where Guruji[18] performed an initiation ceremony. A strong storm wind blew up just as he said, "May *Viveka*[19], the light of discrimination, dawn in the third eye. May you attain the *Vairagya*[20] consciousness. May the guru work through you to spread the Word. In this initiation, enlightenment means this: that you are given a power of discrimination. Every time, before you do anything, this light will be telling you whether you should do it or not." The initiation ended, and the storm wind stopped as suddenly as it had begun.

Inside I felt stillness, a hush. Ever since preparing for confirmation in Louisiana, reading Yogananda's search for his guru, and being initiated by Adano, I had dreamed of this day. I wrote in my journal, "I can see that the path before me is harder than any struggle I have known, yet I am calm and prepared, for it is the only way for me. It is the only path worth taking. Therefore I will climb this great mountain knowing that I am in God: God climbing God's mountain." This is the converse of the conventional belief that a spark of divinity (the soul) resides in each of us. It is the idea that somehow all the matter and energy and consciousness of the whole universe is itself the Divine Being. I existed in "It" like a cell exists inside my body: I had a function to perform that was part of the workings of the whole; I was a small element in the great scheme of things.

---

[18] An affectionate personal form of address to one's guru. Adding "ji" to any Sanskrit word is like adding "dear" to the word.

[19] The power to distinguish the Eternal Self from the false self—the ego.

[20] The power to be dispassionate, to face problems boldly, and to perform one's duty without attachment.

I saw enough miracles on the pilgrimage to convince me that the miraculous does exist in the midst of the world we live in, and to reassure me of the reality of other dimensions not normally detected by the senses. The miracles began as we were flying into Bombay at the very beginning of the trip. As incredible as it sounds, I distinctly saw the form of a young man melt through the left wall of the airplane, walk across the cabin, and melt through the wall on the right side. The entire trip continued with sustaining doses of wonder just when I seemed to need them most. I

Keshavadas blessing me in the Ganges

gave up looking for miracles when the eyes of a statue of Panduranga opened, and shot forth a burst of rainbow brilliance. The miraculous just began to seem normal after that.

Keshavadas laughed indulgently at my thirst for miracles, and had once cryptically remarked, "You do not know with whom you're walking." I took this to mean that his moment-to-moment consciousness of the Divine was a greater miracle than the wonders I sought. This did not feel condescending or arrogant on his part, as much as a statement of where I was on my path. I felt understood by him and completely acknowledged as a dearly loved spiritual son. I was relieved and full of joy, as if finally a deep emotional need was satisfied that my own father could not fulfill. Keshavadas was at the pinnacle in my pantheon: he was the one who was introducing me to God. Although his fame in the world was far in the background for me, I saw literally thousands of devotees who flocked to him as a guru, and I gradually learned he was a world famous author, composer, and teacher who consulted with prime ministers and popes. With such a spiritual father, it seemed possible that I could achieve self-realization and contribute to world peace.

Returning to Texas, I faced the tremendous conflict of continuing with my job and my profession versus devoting myself entirely to Keshavadas' work at one of his centers. As I ruminated over what to do, I became depressed and lifeless. Just before I quit my job to become a full-time devotee, I felt a tremendous surge of energy when I realized that I had to live the life I had created, not change to a new one. This felt good, so I went farther. Perhaps I was where I was in order to share the tremendous healing power of devotional chanting with the world of psychology. My aspirations were, after all, not so far from the ideals I had learned from my mother's adulation of Albert Schweitzer, and my training in Western psychology could certainly link with mantras in the service of noble intentions and transformation.

As this revelation settled in, I decided I needed two things to go on this path. One was expensive, but within my reach: the heavy gold, silver, and copper bracelets that Adano made according to Yogananda's description for balancing the astrological and energetic influences on the body. I felt they would help stabilize my sensitivity to the intense emotions that were intrinsic to my work. The other need I recognized was for a life partner, a committed relationship with a beautiful, spiritual, sensual woman. It had been three years since my divorce, and I had sown enough wild oats to recognize that sensational sex was not enough to keep me happy. I wanted sensational sex in a stable, spiritually fulfilling relationship. I asked Adano to make the bracelets, and I decided to seize the next opportunity to talk to Keshavadas about a life partner.

58

# *Searching for My Soul Mate*

On the pilgrimage I had begun to get to know Keshavadas' life partner, Rama Mata, a sincere and radiantly pure woman with a voice like a nightingale. Having been blessed with three children in their earlier years, they were now dedicated full time to spreading the songs of the saints and the messages of the masters. They seemed to me to be an ideal Hindu Brahmanic couple living in chastity and celibacy after raising a family. Seeing their relationship, I realized very clearly that for me this ideal placed too much distance between spirit and sex. I wanted to integrate sexual intensity, emotional intimacy, and spiritual companionship—and my deepest self-awareness told me that I needed to do it. I somehow knew that having a soul mate with whom to share physical passion, emotional storms, and spiritual aspirations was necessary for me to fulfill my destiny.

However, this was far from the reality of my relationships. On the passionate extreme, I seemed relentlessly attracted to sexy women, from colleagues to go-go dancers, none of whom were interested in an ongoing commitment with me. In the middle ground, I had many wonderful female friends whom I could not imagine as a partner and who were not sexually attracted to me. On the non-passionate extreme were women friends who were attracted to me and whom I rejected as partners. Although I was afraid to hurt their feelings, I had to make it clear that I wanted them to cool it and keep our relationship platonic.

All things considered, I felt I needed Keshavadas' support in preparing myself for a life partner who was both sexy and holy. He gave me a mantra for partnership[21] with a beautiful wife, who was devoted to truth, and who could help me across the ocean of this life and the ones to come. Wearing my new astrological lightning rod

---

[21] For partnership with a woman, *Patneem Manoramam Dehi* means, "Oh, god, bless me with a beautiful wife who is obedient to truth." The mantra for partnership with a man, *Sat Patim Dehi* means, "Oh, God, bless me with a godly husband."

bracelets, I began an intense mantra *sadhana*[22] under a total eclipse of the full moon in July 1981. I stared at the progression of the earth's shadow across the face of the moon, and then sat meditating for hours under the blazing moonlight. All in all this combination must have been an overload. I soon got sick, developed a skin rash, and felt depressed and overwhelmed. However, I was determined to carry on with this life-transforming project.

For months, I found it almost impossible to concentrate on the mantra. I sensed that some unconscious aspects of my psyche had a very strong resistance to its vibration. It seemed the only way I could focus was to chant while jogging. On Keshavadas' next trip to Houston, I spoke about this difficulty. He encouraged me to sit down and focus myself, but was very tolerant of my struggle. Gradually I shifted to more sitting and less jogging, and I began to feel that the mantra was sending a signal from all levels of my being to my soul mate. Somehow I knew I would find her.

Although I certainly did not do the mantra sadhana perfectly in any strict sense, I continued chanting it as sincerely as I could, and the image of my partner-to-be evolved. I knew that however right she was for me in other ways, I needed to feel turned-on to her physically, to trust that she was secure in herself emotionally and materially, and to respect her as a spiritual seeker. The comic book version of my goddess was a rich angel-witch with a cute ass. In my more evolved moments I vibrated the mantra in each chakra, in order to heal the emotional issue associated with that area of the body.

The first round of seven repetitions was especially for the first *chakra*[23], so I focused attention thereby gently tensing my anal sphincter, then chanted my way up all seven steps. The second cycle of seven was dedicated to healing the sex center, so I focused and tensed the genitals before beginning this set of repetitions. This continued up all seven chakras. It felt like a warm, gentle wave of healing proceeding up my body. I used my mala while doing this meditation of seven cycles of seven

---

[22]  Program of spiritual practice.

[23]  Vortex of energy linking the soma, psyche, and spirit. On the physical level, it corresponds to the endocrine glands, whose hormonal secretions regulate our lives. Literally, "wheel," in Sanskrit.

repetitions, then continued to chant fifty-nine more repetitions to make a total of one hundred eight. I usually began by chanting out loud with a full voice, sometimes continuing out loud until the very end, sometimes continuing silently. I followed my intuition.

| chakra | location | issue |
|--------|----------|-------|
| 7 | crown | cosmic connection |
| 6 | brow center | intuition |
| 5 | throat | communication |
| 4 | heart center | love |
| 3 | solar plexus | power |
| 2 | genitals | sexuality |
| 1 | anus | survival |

After about seven months of this meditation, a friend told me about a woman who was on a spiritual quest, did yoga, and ate as weird as I did. I was interested. Even more interesting, all at once I began hearing her name from other people. Another friend asked me to do a radio interview with him, and then at the last minute invited Rickie Moore instead. When a third friend planned a gathering of mental health professionals interested in the future of our city, I checked the invitation list and found her name. I knew the mantra was working. I chanted non-stop as I drove to the meeting, and felt a delicious calm as I parked my car. The April full moon watched through the trees as I made my way to the door.

# IV. Abundance

*I give you the most precious gift of all: I give you love. I give you
care and protection. I commit to encouraging your search for personal freedom and your exploration for truth. I give you absolute
forgiveness and an open heart. I give you honesty. I commit to never
betraying or abandoning you, or leaving you hurting. I shall love
all other women/men as sisters/brothers. I take you as my life partner, as a constant image of Goddess/God in woman/man. I take
your hand in friendship and love.*

Rickie Moore

## A Rose by Any Other Name

Sitting among the friends and colleagues whom I considered the finest people in the
ranks of Houston's mental health professionals, Rickie Moore stood out like a rose
among lilies. She glowed with an almost palpable radiance. As the group took turns
introducing themselves, I learned that she had her Ph.D. in counselling psychology,
and was highly respected as a psychotherapist. From the first moment she spoke, it
was clear that she had an electrifying presentation and important things to say. She
had had a variety of careers that included being a model, a housewife, an advertising
executive, and manager of a dinner theater. She had two grown daughters and a

private practice, and was eager to move on to whatever was next in her life. Later that evening while our colleagues discussed mental health issues, Rickie and I danced and made our way out into the moonlight to say goodnight in private. We acknowledged the romantic potential with a brief kiss, and focused on our mutual delight in having found a colleague who knew that however useful our psychological methods might be, they are incomplete if they leave out the spirit.

I floated home very excited. It was clear to me the instant we met that my prayers had been answered, but I had not acknowledged that to her within those first few hours. I was confident that I could easily tell her when we were private and had more time. Perhaps she already knew this because she was extremely intuitive and had mentioned that she frequently experienced what she called "angelic guidance." This evening I had simply said that after three years of single life and a lot of experimentation, I felt ready for partnership and that I had been working on this for months with a mantra.

When we met for dinner a few nights later and shared more details, it quickly became clear to both of us that I felt very open to a deep relationship with her, but that she felt pretty cautious about a deep relationship with anybody. Actually, this frank sharing about our lives made it easy for both of us to relax and enjoy the relationship regardless of how it developed. I somehow knew we were made for each other, and figured she would sooner or later feel that way, too. I just needed to take care not to push her or threaten to limit her freedom. I kept chanting the mantra, and remembered Keshavadas' words, "Do your best. Leave the rest to God." In this case it felt like, "Leave the rest to Goddess."

From my psychological training, I knew when you try hard to get someone to love you and you succeed, you often become depressed because you do not feel loved for who you are, but rather for what you did. Similarly, I reasoned it is not a good idea to try hard to get results from a mantra. Just surrender to the vibration and let the mantra do its work. From an Eastern perspective this is easy, because the spiritual ideal is to surrender the ego. However, in the West our psychological ideal to develop the ego makes us inclined to try harder rather than to surrender. My intention was to chart a middle course: develop the ego (how I relate to the world) by acknowledging that there is something bigger than I am. It was my version of affirming that the world was round, even though it might look flat. This helped me stay relaxed in the early stages of the relationship, so that when I chanted the partnership mantra it was with the intention of letting the vibration attune both of us to whatever was truly the highest good.

As a result, I could say to Rickie, "Let's allow our relationship to take whatever form supports each of us on our individual paths in life, rather than compromise our individual quests for truth in order to have the relationship look a certain way." We committed ourselves to this. It expressed my truth and quieted her concerns, and on we went deliriously happy, with our love growing more each day. We spent more and more time together, and though I kept my own apartment, I almost always stayed at her town house.

From the beginning of our relationship, I shared mantras with Rickie to improve the quality of our time together. When we spent days apart, I put her picture on my altar and chanted to feel in contact. When we were together and felt out of harmony or wanted to connect deeply, we would chant a mantra to get on the same wavelength. *Om Gam Ganapatayae* was and is the mantra we used most often for this.

The subject of the mantra *Ganapatayae* (or *Ganesh*) is the Lord of All Beings and the Lord of Tantra, who has a special closeness to lovers who intend to experience the Divine through their erotic love. Chanting this mantra helps us remember that the sexual partner is an image of God, and that honoring and loving the other is worship. Ganesh is also the Lord of Beginnings and Remover of Obstacles, so this mantra is also appropriate for beginning any new activity or for removing obstacles to your noble intentions. Chanting the same mantra in so many daily experiences-beginning the day, before making love, going on a journey, when stuck in traffic-brings a unity to life by associating each episode with high consciousness.

We also chanted other mantras. *Sat Nam*[24] was often used in yoga classes we attended: during exercises, meditations, and to close the session. We frequently use it in daily life to acknowledge an important event, or before eating. More recently we have begun chanting *Dhanyavad*[25] before eating. Chanting before eating is not only

---

[24] To honor the truth in oneself, in the other, in the situation. Literally it means, "Truth is the name."

[25] To say, "Thank you," and to feel gratitude. Literally it means, "Blessed thanks and bliss."

a way of pausing to honor the cook (a very good idea in itself). It charges the food with the noble intention of the mantra and readies the body, mind, and spirit to receive maximum nourishment.

We were very aware of the vibrational quality of the names we called each other. We usually called each other "Honey" or "Sweetheart" because our given names were the ones we used out in the world with every one else, and did not seem to express the special feelings we felt for each other. We often called each other "Dr. Moore" and "Dr. Marshall" as a joking way of accepting the other's authority, as in, "Right away, Dr. Moore," or, "Yes, sir, Dr. Marshall."

When Rickie met Keshavadas he immediately gave her the spiritual name Satya which means "Truth." Keshavadas had given me the name Himawantadas, which means "Servant of the Spirit of the Mountain." I particularly liked "Himawan," the short form of the name Keshavadas sometimes used for me. However, the full name was a little clumsy on my lips, and did not appeal to Rickie. She proposed asking him to give me a new name. I was feeling like a new person in our relationship, and the idea of a new spiritual name felt fine to me. When she asked him during his next visit to Houston, Keshavadas chuckled and said, "Yes, a good name for Henry is Dharmaraj, King of Dharma (righteous action)." Rickie liked it, and I did, too. We both felt the names Satya and Dharmaraj expressed who we really are and who we aspire to be. Her life is all about telling the truth, just as mine is about doing the right thing.

The vibration of Sanskrit carries the meaning of the word; in fact the vibration is the meaning, like in a mantra. In this sense we invoked the divine qualities of truth and righteous action by pronouncing our names. We discovered that these spiritual names were especially useful if we were having a difficult time with each other. Addressing her by her spiritual name called out to her divinity and even in an argument would invariably jolt her to a higher consciousness. When she called me Dharmaraj, I wanted to live up to my name.

Every day brought new revelations of the power of the Goddess who lived in the world as Dr. Rickie Moore[26]. She was an exceptional therapist; wise, funny, and sensitive with

---

[26] To avoid confusion, she is referred to as "Rickie" in this text.

friends and family; a skilled and knowledgeable explorer of consciousness.

I had to be careful not to belittle her when I did not feel that I was great enough to be her partner. Staying curious helped a lot when I felt threatened by her power.

Then I remembered that in my mantra meditations for a partner, I had often focused on the idea that I was searching for someone "at least as evolved, dedicated, and committed as myself." I could not help but laugh when I realized how pompous this sounded. I could imagine God and the angels chuckling, "The white male doctor wants a partner at least his equal. OK, let's give him what he wants, with some extra magnificence just to shake him up!" This ironic awareness helped me stay curious and surrender to the loving wisdom expressed by Rickie, even if we were having a hard time of it with heated words or hurt feelings.

Satya and Dharmaraj

The mantra for a female partner *Patneem Manoramam Dehi* invokes *Durga*, the regal *Shakti* (goddess power) associated with destruction of ignorance. Like the fangs of the lioness which rip her prey but gently cradle her cubs when she carries them, Durga's power rips the ego and gently cradles the soul (Keshavadas, 1976a). Considering all this helped a lot when I felt threatened by Rickie's anger or assertiveness or magnificence. After all, I had asked for her, the Universe had given her to me, and she was ripping up my ego for my own good.

Most of the time our relationship was far above the sabotage attempts of my competitive-male-ego demons. We simply had too much fun to stay stuck in problems. We were both food fanatics, but we ate differently. She ate low fat, low salt, low sugar, also basically vegetarian. I ate solar, combining different foods depending on the time of day, and basically vegetarian. Each of us had a lot of variety if we were eating on our own, but our options were very limited if we wanted to have a meal together at home. Our friends joked that if we both strictly followed our dietary restrictions, we would only eat hot filtered water dosed with cayenne pepper.

Rather than get stuck in, "My food is better than yours," we stayed curious and combined our knowledge. We realized we could relax our diets and still enjoy the health benefits they had brought us, if we each drank our own morning urine and applied it to the skin. This would give the chemical biofeedback effect of eating solar, recycle hormones, and be great for the complexion. We kept a pee-drinking glass in the bathroom (washed after every use), and encouraged each other by commenting on our youthful-looking skin. We also laughed a lot and began to enjoy eating well together.

Gradually we even learned how to work together. We were both mental health professionals, but we have very different talents. She is a brilliant therapist, counsellor, and group leader with dramatic shamanistic intuition. I am a careful diagnostician and clinician with a passion for devotional healing mantras. On the dark side, she thinks she can do anything and I think I know it all. Rather than get stuck in, "My way is better than yours," we stayed flexible and cooperated. I covered her private practice in Houston while she began to lead workshops in Europe. She opened a new universe of creative therapeutic possibilities in the workshops, and eventually invited me to assist and ground her energetically when the demands of the workshops overtaxed her psychic sensitivity. Somewhere along the way she even persuaded me to change my hairstyle, buy new clothes, and lighten-up—much to the delight of my friends and clients.

When Rickie began leading workshops in Europe, I shifted my psychological work from emotionally disturbed school children to hospitalized pain patients. This gave me more income, more flexible work hours, and more time to cover her practice when she was away. As I changed the form of my professional work, I risked sharing more of my spiritual life with colleagues, and expressed my enthusiasm for the psychological benefits of mantras.

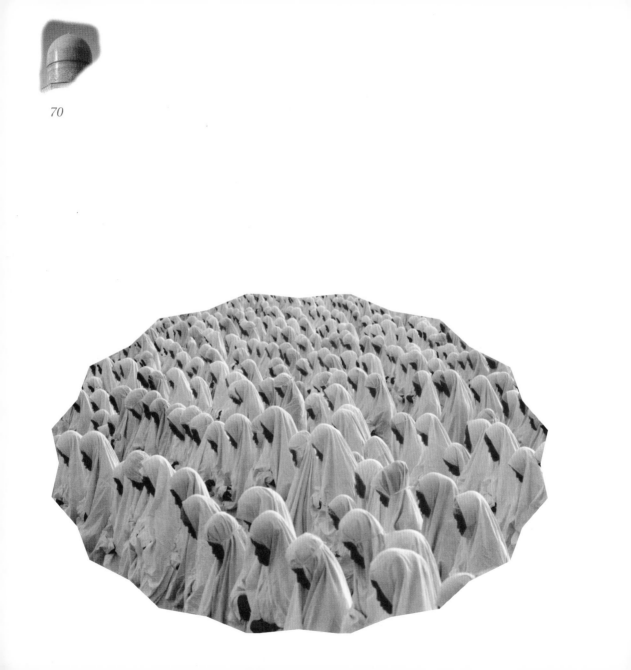

# *Beyond the Dangling Conversation*

A skeptical colleague in the hospitals often questioned my beliefs of how mantras helped with my financial problems or supported me in finding a partner. She assumed that any physical or psychological improvements I had experienced were due to my wish to believe, rather than to any real effects of the practice itself (a "placebo effect").

I knew that it was well documented and fairly well accepted that positive expectations correlate with positive outcomes for psychological and medical treatment. A lot of research shows that positive imagery, such as imagining medicine eating up cancer cells, helps people get better results from chemotherapy. At this time (in the mid-1980s) we knew that it was likely that a behavioral treatment, such as relabeling compulsive urges rather than giving in to them, could have a measurable effect on the brain, very similar to what medication does.[27]

"Brain and mind are inseparable, two ways of looking at the same thing," I argued. "Sounds from a doctor's voice or from a mantra send vibrations along the neurons to the brain. There's no reason why these sonic oscillations could not redirect the flow of neurotransmitters the way a manufactured drug does, maybe in even better ways. It's clear that with the brain thus altered, different signals are sent to the body and behavior is changed."

After I concluded my scientific apologia, she gave me a skeptical look and said, "Exploring an ancient Eastern technology for using sound vibrations to make the mind calm is too exotic. Why not just use a nice relaxation tape and get on with living here and now?"

"The potential benefits of applying mantras to daily life are the chance of a lifetime," I insisted. "If they only focused the mind and promoted regular deep breathing, they would enhance health. But they also fill awareness with positive messages,

---

[27]    Conclusively demonstrated in the mid-1990s.

diminish worry, and give relief from the overload of negativity we are exposed to every day. That makes them a great healing tool. They could be compared to other relaxation and positive affirmation methods. It's a simple matter of which methods get better results. That's totally scientific."

She nodded and asked, "But can you let science make a verdict about the efficacy of mantras based on such simple comparison studies?"

I paused and shook my head. "Not really. In my heart of hearts I feel there's something more, something about the vibration itself that transmits the positive effects."

She frowned and said, "Sounds like you believe the magic just cannot be studied, and that's unacceptable to a scientist. I've heard that mantras come from the ancient oral traditions of the Himalayan region. They were written down in the Vedas, practiced in the ceremonies of Hinduism, and passed orally from guru to disciple for thousands of years. Why cannot you just let it go at that, and study it as a body of knowledge? What's all the mystery?"

I smiled, "I guess for me the mystery is that the origin of mantras is in transcendent states of consciousness. Although people often assume that mantras exist as a body of assigned phrases and melodies, this is not the whole story. Mantras exist in this form today because they have been preserved in a guru-disciple tradition. This tradition asserts that such a mantra originated as inspired utterance or sound heard in a great sage's meditation. Other mantras are simply more recent developments of the guru-disciple tradition, which is alive and well in the present day. Gurus pass on the ancient mantras plus ones they have discovered, and thereby introduce their initiates to heightened states of consciousness. The initiates, in turn, have their own experiences with mantras, which they pass on to the next generation. This continues in the present. It means that ancient mantras, as well as newly discovered ones, all link normal consciousness to transcendent states."

"I hear what you're saying," she nodded. "It's extreme, but it is plausible that an experience that led to a mantra could be accessed by chanting that mantra. However, the notoriety of gurus like Bhagwan Rajneesh and his Rolls Royces is going to make it very hard for people to take seriously your trust in gurus. The whole guru-disciple tradition seems such a set up for charlatans to take advantage of gullible dependent followers."

I had to breathe deep and acknowledge what she said. "There's no arguing that. However every profession, including ours, has been used to defraud the public at one time or other."

"Come on!" she challenged, laughing. "There's no ethics code or professional standards committees for gurus. There is a difference." When I nodded, she continued, asking, "So cons and charisma aside, why is it preferable to get a mantra from a guru, rather than through procedures normal for Western people like looking it up in a book, going to school, or doing research?"

I said, "The idea behind the custom is that mantras are traditionally given directly by a teacher to a student to transmit an actual vibration. Of course, emotionally it's an empowerment based in a relationship of deep trust and mutual respect. However," I added, "I would not rule out non-direct methods. I have a very stable, dependable friend who swears he had a transcendent experience reading a book by Swami Muktananda. I certainly have my own remarkable experiences reading Yogananda, and chanting with Keshavadas' tapes."

She was getting more interested. "It seems intuitively obvious that the ideal would be that a mantra comes from a guru who practices what he preaches, and goes directly to a sincere and inquisitive disciple, who really practices spiritual disciplines. However, if the vibration were really the essence, then a recording would work. At least that begins to sound measurable."

"Yes," I agreed. "Transmission of mantra vibrations has definitely gone beyond the direct-contact, guru-disciple relationship because now teachers can record mantras. I have continued to learn from Keshavadas through his recordings. That has tremendous advantages over reading text because the sound vibration is the essential point, not the written character. If the sound of a recorded mantra touches you deeply, you can rely on this experience, whether or not you actually meet the teacher transmitting the vibration. Of course, relying on your own best pronunciation of a printed mantra text would be better than no mantra at all. However, I would surely encourage anybody reading a mantra in a book to contact the writer and hear the vibration."

"So," she mused, "mantras are magical mystical words that do not totally defy scientific study?"

I agreed, saying, "I cannot adequately express my experience of mantras with the linear language of logic. It's more a feeling than a thought. Explanations seem to run in circles. There are so many metaphysical levels in Eastern teachings, and mantras have applications at all of them. It's like peeling the cosmic onion: you never get to the core. In its highest meaning, mantra is a word that takes the person who sincerely chants it across the ocean of rebirth. At a lower level, it is an occult formula to remove various troubles or to fulfill various mundane desires, depending on the motives with which the mantra is chanted. In another sense, mantras are prayers that invoke the deities presiding over nature, whose grace bring health and healing. What is fundamental to all these definitions is that mantra is word power. 'In the beginning was the Word,'[28] and all that."

My colleague laughed, looked at her watch and got ready to go to an appointment. "Our hospital administrator would have a heart attack and fundamentalists would be up in arms if they heard your patients were praying to Hindu gods for a magical cure."

"Is not that the truth," I laughed with her "and plenty of our patients and staff are just about that conservative."

"OK. So you're not going to be doing any magical incantations in the staff lounge anytime soon?" she kidded.

"You can count on it, and I promise not to write any chart notes in Sanskrit."

As we parted, I was careful to conclude with a few reassurances about patient care being the priority of my work. In Houston's hospitals, it was more acceptable to be preoccupied with golf or money than with metaphysics, and I did not want to become the target of ultra-conservatives. In fact, mantras were too exotic for most of my pain patients' conservative Southern Christian backgrounds, so I chanted on

---

[28]    John, 1:1

their behalf without telling them, and otherwise used conventional pain management techniques with them.

I traveled from one hospital to the next, zoomed through Houston traffic playing mantras in my car at full volume, chanted at the top of my lungs, and soared into Heaven until I pulled into the next hospital parking lot. Then, charged with cosmic vibrations, I would enter the hospital as a medical psychologist with my brief case and white coat to help the patients as best I could. I did not analyze or question how the mantras may have helped my patients. I just knew that the mantras helped me, because by being more centered and clear, I was also becoming more effective. I did not imagine that these qualities would soon be needed by Rickie far more urgently than by my patients.

# *Ghost Buster*

I was neck deep in the hospital scene and chanting mantras to keep from drowning, when Rickie returned exhausted from doing two five-day workshops in Europe. I picked her up at the airport, and she told me about her experiences as we drove to our home. She was preoccupied with a woman who had come to the last workshop complaining of depression and plagued with frequent petite mal epileptic seizures. The woman's depression had lifted and the frequency and severity of her seizures had dramatically diminished. But Rickie was afraid she had somehow picked up her client's tics and mannerisms. As she told me this, I could see that she was terrified. My heart pounded with alarm, but I stayed supportive, hoping that rest and tender loving care would help her come around. I suggested that we take a hot bath as soon as we got home, and promised I'd give her a massage. Rickie was vague and distant during the bath, and got very dizzy when we got out of the tub. By the time I helped her to the bed her face was grimaced, her eyes were rolled up in her head, and her body was contorted with spastic gestures. I held her tight until she quieted down and her breathing slowed. Clearly this was far too serious to handle with massage, snuggling, or bed rest. Hospitalization was out of the question, and I had already intervened about as much as could be hoped for with crisis psychotherapy.

Then I remembered a mantra. I told my still-trembling sweetheart that I would do a banishing mantra[29] to clear negativity and evil influences. As she lay in bed, I sat beside her and my booming voice and handclaps shattered the silence. The atmosphere instantly changed. I repeated the mantra three times, as Keshavadas had taught. Each repetition came stronger than the last. The final clap with the final syllable

---

[29] To use the mantra *Hum Phut Sva Ha*, first inhale deep. Then intone a loud deep sound, *Hum* (rhymes with "zoom"), while contracting the solar plexus. Without taking in any more breath, make three deep penetrating sounds, *Phut Sva Ha* (rhymes with "foot cha cha"), giving each sound the same emphasis. At the precise moment of uttering each of the three final sounds, clap hands sharply and loudly over the head.

rang through the air like a roar of triumph. My hair stood on end and I felt ice cold. Rickie breathed out a deep sigh, took my hand, and whispered, "She's gone."

After this incredible experience, I realized there was no way it was safe for Rickie to lead a workshop of forty people, assisted only by a translator and an organizer. She agreed. The five-day-and-night workshops were almost nonstop marathons, and her intuitive therapeutic style left her vulnerable to taking on the problems of her clients. She became a psychic sponge and absorbed the negativity she so successfully helped others release. To continue this powerful style of work, she needed to be grounded and shielded from this negativity. I wanted to help her, I was excited to participate in this work, and I was good as a ghost buster. I often used mantras for centering and protection, and I further stabilized my energy by wearing an initiation mala from Keshavadas and the astrological bracelets made by Adano. Working together promised to be a completely natural solution. We excitedly planned that I would take time away from medical psychology in order to assist her at her next series of workshops.

In the groups I sat beside Rickie as she led the activities. I saw to it that I maintained body contact with her whenever she interacted intensely with a group member. During these times, I concentrated on a mantra and sent energy through my hands into her. The workshops were filled with humor, fun, and love. However, when deep release and healing took place, the atmosphere became intense. During these times, silently chanting mantras and supporting my partner in her role as group leader, I delighted in my new role as workshop ghost buster. The results were good: Rickie said she never felt better at the end of the workshops. However, we soon noticed that I was pretty wiped out by the experience. The intensity of the workshops required that we learn something else.

It sounded incredible to go to a psychic consultant, and I half-expected somebody to float into the room claiming to channel alien entities. But my resistance relaxed as I listened to the no-nonsense approach of the clear-eyed young man who was trained in physics and engineering. His questions made it clear that while grounding Rickie in the workshop, I had been concentrating at my brow center as I normally did while chanting a mantra. He said this focus overloaded the subtle energy channels of my upper chakras by giving them a job for which they were not designed. He advised me that for this work I should stay grounded and focused on the lower centers at the anus, genitals, and solar plexus. This would activate the far larger and stronger energy channels that are designed for survival, safety, and power. This advice felt right, and it worked beautifully.

Shifting my awareness to the pelvic region made me aware of the pulse there. When I squeezed my anus, genitals, and belly in rhythm with it, I felt as if I could "pump" this pulsing life energy out of my hands into Rickie while she was working with someone. Depending on how she was standing, moving, or sitting with the client, I positioned myself behind her and kept my hands firmly on her lower back, hips, or heels. By mentally chanting in rhythm with my pelvic pulse, I stayed strong and centered while keeping her safe.

The mantras I typically used in this situation were *Om Ham Hanumate* (for victory, strength, and healing), *Om Gam Ganapatayae* (to remove obstacles), or *Om Dum Durgayai / Om Kreem Kaalikayai* (to protect from negative influences). I silently chanted these mantras in a monotone with emphasis on the *bija* or seed syllable, which contains the power of the entire mantra, i.e., *Ham*, *Gam*, *Dum*, or *Kreem* respectively. These mantras became wonderful safe havens in high stress situations.

I assisted Rickie like this in several workshops before I offered to lead a mantra chanting session one morning. Rickie was interested and asked, "What mantra would you chant?" *Om Sri Ram Jai Ram Jai Jai Ram* seemed perfect to both of us: it was simple and melodious, and it had an energy that brought victory to the power of love. However, I did not play a musical instrument when I chanted, and some accompaniment was needed to help the group stay together. We discussed different ideas. I had studied piano for years as a child and felt comfortable with the possibility of using a harmonium. Keshavadas played a harmonium[30] when he sang and chanted before groups, and I was familiar with the instrument. We decided to find an

---

[30] Indian musical instrument, somewhat similar in size and construction to an accordion, having keys and air pump mechanism, but played sitting on the floor and making a deep, rich tone.

Indian music shop to see what was available. The harmoniums we found seemed a little bulky, and I was drawn to their smaller cousin: a shruti box[31]. It made steady tones that could be varied by covering different openings with the fingers, and it folded to the size of a large book when not in use. I fell in love with its rich harmonics and was confident that with a little practice I could lead mantra chanting in a workshop.

When I did chant *Rama Mantra* in a workshop, even though most participants had never heard of mantras—much less chanted one—the group was enthusiastic. They wanted to chant the next morning and the next. After that, we offered mantra chanting each morning after yoga. A couple of people in almost every workshop asked if there were mantras that could help them with specific problems. Thus began a new phase in my experience of mantras: teaching.

---

[31] Literally means "heard" in Sanskrit. A shruti box makes sounds that can be heard.

# *The Magic of Love*

When I excitedly told Keshavadas about teaching the workshop group a mantra, he looked me in the eyes, put his hand on my head, and said, "Dharmaraj, you are blessed to teach the mantras. You and Satya will help to heal many people through the power of mantras."

This blessing thrilled me, and I dived into the ten or so mantras Keshavadas had given me, to determine which would be appropriate for our groups. For several years since meeting Keshavadas, I had mainly used mantras he had taught me that were complex and required initiation and rigorous spiritual practice (sadhana). I felt they were much too demanding for me to share in a group. When I selected mantras to chant in the workshops, I was often torn between my desire to chant complicated mantras one hundred eight times, and the group's need for mantras they could learn quickly and chant for a shorter time. My conflict was resolved when my intentions were clear: my job, my joy, and my privilege was to share with the group the power and wonder of mantras. The joy of group members chanting together, their shining faces and peaceful smiles, was absolutely apparent when they could relax into a mantra. When the group struggled with a difficult text or a complex melody, they never really reached the experience the mantra was intended to give.

After a workshop in Austria, Cindy Freedman, a wonderfully talented musician who had played and sung in the workshop, summed it up. When I asked about her experience, she looked at me with her huge, clear eyes and said, "I love chanting mantras with you when my mind is able to turn off, and I get high on the experience. That's what it's about for me. If the mantra's too complicated, my mind never stops, and I feel frustrated. Then the next time we chant mantras, I'm more resistant. I want to have a transcendent experience every time I chant."

This wonderful feedback gave me the determination to keep the mantras simple in order to satisfy group members' hunger for transcendence. It let me accept that technique and ritual are detrimental if they interfere with devotion and surrender. I made a commitment to chant full-heartedly and for as long as it felt intuitively right, and to only chant a predetermined number of repetitions when there was a compelling reason. As I relaxed my preconceptions, I could see that longer periods of chanting were well suited to relieving physical and emotional distress, while briefer periods gave emotional satisfaction and brought inner peace. In any case, the key was to chant from the heart.

Opening my heart let me enjoy and appreciate many more facets of Rickie's creative capacities. I actually felt turned on by her power, and she blossomed with the acknowledgment. She encouraged and guided workshop participants to create a strong support system for solving problems. She integrated mantras with yogic and shamanic methods she already used, and deepened her ability to awaken spiritual consciousness. She invited musicians to assist in the work and collaborated with them to compose beautiful songs in four languages, which let the groups dance, sing, and meditate their way to inner peace. In a flash of insight, she decided to change the name of the groups to better acknowledge the balance between deep therapeutic personal work and lighthearted fun. "Workshops sounds like work," she said. "They should be called Playshops—Inner Peace Playshops!" She called her integration of essential healing wisdom "Tri-Energetics,"[32] and soon a number of people who had been to many Playshops wanted to be trained to help others with these methods. In response to this, we began what grew into a Tri-Energetic Counsellor Training, with graduates helping people in seven countries.

As dazzled as I was by her achievements, I was enthralled with her as a partner. I had never known such intimacy and enjoyment. My life's quest was to have transcendent experiences, ongoing face-to-face experience of God. For most of my life I had imagined this was essentially a solitary quest, and that it led to inner, private experiences. With Rickie I discovered that magic and divinity need not be separate from daily life; they permeate it. Keshavadas had introduced me to this possibility

---

[32] Therapeutic system which incorporates: the unity of soma, psyche, and spirit; the importance of being flexible, tolerant, and curious; and the formula, "Know what you need, say what you want, and have clear intentions."

on the pilgrimage. Now Rickie and I had lived with divine magic for several years, and I realized that I found the most immediate and sustained experience of the Divine in my Beloved. It was amazing and exciting to feel that God, Herself, was in my life, in my bed, and in my face.

After three years of working and living together, we were ready to celebrate our union in a ceremony. We were satisfied with the commitments we had made over the years to clarify our relationship to ourselves and to others. We had begun our relationship with an agreement that we both could have sexual relations with other people, and that we would always let the other know what was going on (this was in the early 1980s when we thought we could not catch anything that could not be cured by penicillin). Pretty soon we discovered that although we liked the idea of sexual freedom, we both felt more comfortable with a monogamous relationship, so that became our commitment. In order not to complicate open, loving relationships in our groups with sexual feelings, it became more important for us to commit to not flirt or play sexual games with others.

These commitments protected the rights of each of us to stay close to dear friends, former partners, and even former lovers. They let us feel secure that no other relationship threatened our partnership. We each needed to feel loved by others, and we accepted that getting turned on and fantasizing was normal, healthy, and our right. We just agreed that sexually we would, "Shop all over town, but eat dinner at home." Opening our hearts and minds and bodies to each other allowed us to explore sacred sexuality. Acknowledging that my most passionate urges are the well spring of my spiritual life, and celebrating this with my partner was a big step in the process of healing a split that runs through Eastern and Western cultures, straight to the core of the individual. It felt great to be sexy and holy.

In the summer of 1985, we married in a spiritual ceremony with Keshavadas in California, went to a tantra workshop as a honeymoon holiday in Mexico, then had a church ceremony with our family and friends in Houston. We committed ourselves to see the other as a constant image of God/Goddess. I committed to seeing other women as sisters and she to seeing other men as brothers. This let us relax and love other people without any hanky-panky.

Spiritual patnership ceremony with Keshavadas

# V. Mission

*Separation from community is clearly related to the assumption that we are separate from the earth. It has not only the same philosophical cause—the overriding faith in the power of the individual intellect—but also the same solution: a more balanced way of thinking about our relationship to the world, including our communities. This reaffirmation of our connection to others involves an obligation to join with others....*

Al Gore (1992)

## Sharing Mantras

Opening my heart to Rickie helped me open my heart to the world and to bring more love into mantra chanting. Even though I had accepted that groups in the Playshops could not experience a mantra's magic unless the text was simple and the melody memorable, it was difficult to try out a mantra on Rickie and stay open to feedback. What if she felt it was too difficult or boring? Even though I completely trusted her feelings about what would work in a Playshop, I was afraid to lose the mantra's magic by simplifying a text or embellishing a melody. I quieted my fears and lowered my defenses by chanting the partnership mantra that had helped me find my beloved in the first place. As I became more secure and less defended, I felt a fresh curiosity and could welcome her creativity.

In the midst of an animated discussion about our next Playshop, it suddenly occurred to me that since a single syllable (or several syllables) carries the potency of a mantra's entire text, chanting only a few syllables of very complex mantras could transmit the entire vibration. It worked perfectly to simplify the lengthy, complex mantra I had chanted for a partner. Rickie was delighted and enthusiastic. The partner mantras *Patneem Manoramam Dehi* and *Sat Patim Dehi* were needed by many couples seeking to improve their relationship, as well as by many single people who wanted to find a partner. Together Rickie and I discovered a melody for these mantras that was more of a love song the group could enjoy, than a heart-rending-call-to-the-beloved that I had originally chanted. The groups loved dividing in two and taking turns: first chanting for a female partner, then for a male, etc. I questioned Keshavadas about this, and he agreed, supporting this creative breakthrough.

With this encouragement, I turned my attention to other devotional chants I had learned from him. I particularly loved the hauntingly melodious *Raghupati Raghava Raja Ram* (also known as Mahatma Gandhi's prayer), which Gandhi is said to have chanted every morning to purify his intentions and to bring non-violent victory to the power of love. I was also fascinated with the ecstatic power of *Kodanda Rama / Hara Hara Ganga*, which sang in my heart and blended in my imagination to invoke the power of love to protect and to work miracles. Unlike mantras that are chanted by groups in unison with strict repetition of the text, these inspired compositions are chanted responsively with the group following the leader through a series of variations.[33] Because all are very complicated in their full-length versions, I adapted them for Westerners by chanting only the chorus and dividing the lines of text in half. Rickie and the group loved them, particularly when we began sweet and soft and built to ecstatic climaxes. This left me pouring with sweat, and the group radiant with joy.

This avalanche of creativity gave me confidence to begin to share with groups the original mantras that from time to time would come to me when I was chanting or

---

[33]  This form is known as *bhajan*.

meditating. One came as my mother neared death, which relieved me of guilt and sadness for not being with her, and let me feel in close, loving contact with her spirit. As my mother struggled through her last days, I wanted to remain in close emotional contact, but found myself seven thousand kilometers from her, struggling to accept the intense feelings that burned in my heart. The silent sad shadow of the woman who gave me life was returning to the Mother of us all.

Sitting alone in the meditation room of a Buddhist Center in Austria, I played my shruti box and chanted, struggling to find some inner peace. Then tears began to flow and a mantra poured from me that I had never heard before. The text and melody came all at once, and I chanted *Jaya Jaya Devi Mata* over and over. It simply meant victory and salutations to the Goddess Mother. I felt I was honoring the divinity in my own mother by honoring Devi Mata. My pain dissolved as I chanted. I felt I was working for the Goddess by helping lead the Playshops and by teaching the mantras. I knew that my mother knew I loved her dearly, even if I was not physically with her. I felt incredible joy and peace, and was very grateful that the mantra had come to me. Rickie and I did manage to reach home the night Mamma died. As a thunderstorm raged and lightning illuminated the sky, she left this world peacefully. She always knew how to make a great exit. Since that time, the mantra has helped heal many people's problems with their mothers.

Another mantra came while I was chanting in the home of a dear friend in Texas. Rickie and I were spending so much time in Europe that she had sold her townhouse in Houston. We had returned to the States to see our families. My boys were ten and thirteen, and I seemed to miss them the most when we were in the States and they were at home with their mother. When Rickie and I were busy with Playshops, our frequent calls to the boys and her daughters kept us in good contact. Now in Texas I had some time off, and my heart ached for my boys.

I went to our room, lit some candles and incense, and began chanting. The drone of the shruti box supported my voice as I repeatedly called out, "Shiva," invoking the consciousness that destroys ignorance, stagnation, and anything counter to the highest good. This evolved into, *Hari Shiva*, which meant shining, radiant, masculine divinity. I was getting a little bored with just chanting these holy words, and added the word, *Om* , the great cosmic vibration. Suddenly, a melody came which gave a form to the chant, *Hari Om Shiva Om / Shiva Om Hari Om / Hari Shiva / Shiva Hari Om*. I chanted it over and over, my melancholy vanished, and I was filled with radiant godly consciousness. I felt masculine, sexy, secure, and sure of my closeness to my boys. The fear that I was not a good enough father disappeared.

Keshavadas was soon in Houston and I requested a private session to ask him about this experience. I wondered what *Hari Om Shiva Om* actually meant at a deeper level. Why had that word pattern come to me? Could it be considered a mantra? Could I teach it to others? Was it a mantra that existed before I chanted it, or had it come into the world through me? Beyond the mechanics of breathing, concentrating, repeating, and singing, what was that reality that mantras opened before me?

Keshavadas smiled and his eyes glowed. He said the text was a beautiful joining of Hari—usually associated with Vishnu the preserver—with Shiva the destroyer. To make such a link is to espouse the unity of all religions, and to look beyond the forms of worship and names of deities. He said this deeper meaning behind my experience of radiant, godly masculinity, indicated past life experiences as a devotee of cosmic religion. It was certainly a mantra to pass on to students.

He said that the consciousness in which a mantra is chanted and the consciousness which mantra chanting produces has two distinct varieties. *Mantra Bhajan* is taking refuge in God, similar to the idea of prayer in the West. *Mantra Kirtan* is an overflowing celebration of being face to face with God, similar to the Western concept of transcendental experience. Yogis recognize many gradations of the superconscious state known as samadhi, when the breath cycle stops and the individual soul and Cosmic Spirit are perceived as identical. The essential point relevant to mantras is that *Mantra Bhajan* can take the devotee to samadhi, and that, after samadhi, *Mantra Kirtan* may pour forth. As we left our private talk to get something to eat, Keshavadas laughed gently and said, "It is good to know these things, Dharmaraj, but it is a greater blessing to have the experience."

I felt very grateful for the guidance and acknowledgment. I relaxed about what to call the exact state of consciousness I reached when chanting mantras. I was having experiences that nourished and healed me, and my intuitive devotional mantras had a place in this inspired tradition. More and more mantras came through me that I shared in the Playshops, and I kept close contact with Keshavadas to check my intuitions with his knowledge.

Whenever I had contact with Keshavadas or Adano, no matter how casual or brief, it was in the context of spiritual development. Perhaps the clarity of this intention was enhanced by the fact that our times together were limited to a few moments on the phone, a few hours in a busy schedule, or a few days at a retreat. These precious direct contacts were supplemented by a feeling of being in intuitive contact whenever I needed them. I found that if I had a question and could formulate it so that it could be answered yes or no, I almost always knew the answer within myself. Usually my questions boiled down to, "Can I do such and such?" and that actually meant, "Is this in my best interest as well as in the interest of the highest good?" The initiations I had received were confirmations that I had the capacity to make this distinction, so it made metaphysical common sense that I would know the answer to such questions. I called on the phone if I wanted specific information or closer contact.

Over our twenty-year relationship, Adano so successfully dodged my adulation with his wry humor that I regarded him as a big brother on the path. With him I had developed an adult-adult relationship. Keshavadas, on the other hand, perfectly fit my images of a spiritual father, with just the right mix of humor, wisdom, love, impatience, health problems, and personality quirks to keep him human. I had a child-parent relationship with him most of the time. When our schedules permitted me to meet him in the United States or Europe, I enjoyed playing the role of adoring child with him. I would give him a little massage or take care of some chore to help him. With Keshavadas, I felt satisfied and happy as a growing spiritual child. Then several critical experiences helped the child grow up.

One was Adano's death in 1989. I heard this incredible story from several of his initiates, and I pass it along as a tribute to my big brother Adano. His body was discovered in the early morning sitting on the toilet at the home of students in Richmond, Virginia. He was left undisturbed for hours because he often went into deep, breathless trances. When the authorities were finally called, they were persuaded to keep his body at room temperature without embalming it. He looked asleep, and his body stayed supple. Knowing Adano, he should have been snoring. The doctor at the morgue kept checking for a heartbeat. After seventy-two hours, initiates gathered,

Adano in his last days

hoping he would just get up. Instead a black butterfly fluttered through the group and disappeared in the sunlight. One week later when his casket was sealed, the body still had no discoloration, no rigor, and smelled like roses. The swami who taught immortality life-styles got his ticket punched after only sixty-four revolutions around the sun. Sat Nam, Adano. A few weeks after his death, I wanted to have some indication that his spirit was available to me, so I focused on him in meditation. His face appeared right in front of me and said, "God don't work for nobody." Typical Adano. I got the reassurance I wanted.

Another critical factor in my growing up has been confronting Sant Keshavadas' human weaknesses. When female friends complained of his sexual overtures, Rickie and I seized a private moment and confronted him. Calmly facing our hurt, anger, and confusion, he said simply, "If you cannot forgive me, you can never forgive yourself." Although we were soothed by the wisdom of his words and comforted by our unconditional love for him, gradually I realized that my adoration of Guruji was a projection of my own dreams and wishes onto him. The halo I saw around him was my own creation. This is not a bad thing. I needed someone to fulfill my yearning for a spiritual teacher who was truly divine. Keshavadas, a tremendously evolved human being, gave me that opportunity. For this I am endlessly grateful. I am also very grateful that I was well along in the process of growing up in relation to him when I had to face this challenge to confront, to understand, and to forgive. My child-like idealization of him could not encompass the disappointment and ambiguity of this situation. I experienced the dilemma of any student overly enamored with the teacher's personality: what to do when teacher's halo wobbles? Get rid of friends who criticize the teacher? Disown the teacher? Become disenchanted with valuable teachings? A spiritually awakened adult ego helped me stay centered and tolerate the ambiguity, continuing to love and respect my wonderful friends and my magnificent teacher.

Another important influence that accelerated my growth to spiritual adulthood has been the opportunity to meet the needs of participants in the Playshops. When they ask for help at turning points in their lives—when someone is ill or dying, when a child is born or baptized, when a couple marries or wants a baby—their urgent sincerity demands that I respond without the hindrance of my child-like ego. Chanting mantras at significant moments satisfies a need for ceremony and meaning, and helps unite us by creating a sense of community. Teaching our students to integrate spiritual practices with therapeutic interventions lets me integrate these two dimensions of my being. My inner student-child-seeker, who struggled to integrate spirit and psychology, matured and joined the professional-adult-clinician in serving others.

# *Building Community*

By the mid-1980s, our Playshop work in Europe became so satisfying that Rickie and I devoted ourselves to it full time, and began establishing our home in Amsterdam. Through this process it gradually became apparent that the loneliness Rickie and I had both experienced as children was part of a pervasive social condition, and that as adults we had an opportunity and an obligation to connect people with one another. We began to refer to this community as "Playshop Family."

When our Playshop Family members began asking for recordings to help them chant at home and musician assistants in Playshops began leading chanting groups between Playshops, I was grateful for the opportunity and did my best not to run to Keshavadas for reassurance. We made our first recordings in the Playshops and later worked in a family member's studio, where we lighted candles and incense and chanted in a circle, ignoring the microphones and equipment as much as possible. With everyone's help, we created the openhearted, relaxed atmosphere of a Playshop. Surely the angels accompanied our mostly-non-professional musicians and singers. Soon the playback began to sound as good to our critical ears as the live chanting had sounded when we were in the midst of it. In autumn 1991, when we were getting close to having recordings we could send out into the world, I met with Keshavadas in Paris and played him portions of our best mix. He looked at me and smiled, "Dharmaraj, make the recording. Teach the mantras. You are blessed to continue."

Over a hundred Playshop Family members from six different countries have been directly involved in making mantra recordings over the past seven years. The resulting compact discs have been enthusiastically received by the rest of the Playshop Family, who share them with their own circles of friends. The recordings are something tangible that showed, "This is what we do in those groups I attend." The compact discs helped define the Family's group identity, not just as special talented people, but also as a sharing community. This is because the mantras are not to be passively appreciated, but to be chanted. The recordings create interest in mantras in the broader community. Mantra chanting has grown in importance as a group activity when family members gather to celebrate birthdays or the full moon, or to solve problems or do yoga.

It is a dream-come-true to be spreading mantras to the thousands of people who have bought our recordings since 1992. While the commercial success is gratifying, it is far more important that people hear and chant mantras. For me it is a labor of love and life work to bring mantras into people's lives, and recordings are simply a wonderful opportunity to do this. It surprises and sustains me that many sincere seekers of truth and curious skeptics write for more information and a schedule of mantra chanting gatherings. A few letters each week has grown into hundreds over the years. They whisper to me that there is a spiritual community-in-the-making,

Getting it right in the studio

sustained in part by a ripple of mantra vibrations, pulsing out into the world.

This community is growing one individual at a time, which feels like the steadiest base for any transformative process.

The community of which I feel a part is clustered around our home in Amsterdam, spreads out across Europe, and extends to the United States. It is a community of friends joined in the intention to develop personally, serve others, and support each other. I am very grateful to be supported in spreading mantras, and also in fulfilling my childhood commitment to plant trees. My European friends encouraged me to plant a forest on my land in Louisiana. When Rickie and I led Playshops in Germany's Black Forest or in nature preserves in Austria, I often thought of my family's land. For years I was pained and shamed by the contrast between meticulously groomed European forests and my land choked with brambles and vines. A lot of mantra chanting and a lot of trust from friends who believed in what is possible, even if it does not appear practical, helped sustain those dreams until solutions emerged and over thirteen thousand trees were planted. Louisiana is not Austria. It has its own sullen, wild charm, and it is becoming more beautiful as my little forest grows.

As I meet people who only know me through the mantra recordings, I am careful to introduce myself as a health professional teaching what he has learned from spiritual seeking. I avoid being seen as a self-proclaimed mantra master or true believer. My intention is that a group chanting mantras is a gathering of equals, with each person experiencing his or her Divinity.

The Dutch culture supports this with a humorous skepticism of anyone who presents himself as better than others, and with a lively tradition of singing together in groups. It is a charming fact of Dutch life to hear people singing in bars, and to see groups singing along in the audience on a television show. Almost every village has a musical association with a building, a marching band, and a choir. In this rich cultural background, singing along with mantras is very natural. As our recordings went out into Holland, we started receiving invitations to chant mantras at community music centers, churches, and personal development centers. Our Playshop Family musicians contributed their talents, and we've had a wonderful time chanting with knowledgeable mantra chanters and first-timers, sometimes in gatherings of hundreds of people.

Leading mantra chanting

I was delighted when several musicians in the Family began to offer mantra chanting evenings in other parts of Holland, as well as in Germany, France, Switzerland, and Austria. They chant mantras they have learned from me, as well as ones that have come to them from other sources. I support their departures from what I have taught them by remembering that the teaching embodied in the mantras is more important than the teacher. This removes my ego as an obstacle to my intention to advance these teachings, and brings me inner peace.

Deflating my self-importance as a teacher supports our evolving community, and is a vital step on my path of self-awareness. By accepting the fact that spiritual teachings are greater than the teachers who teach them, I am more aware that tolerance of diversity is absolutely essential for community. It supports development of consciousness and its expression in acts of love and service.

Having shared my discovery of mantras and the role they play in developing consciousness and in sustaining a glorious relationship with my partner, family, and a growing community, the greatest act of love and service I can perform in this book is to refer you to the mantras themselves. May you chant them and discover your own path to peace. Sat Nam.

# *Appendix A*

## *Sheet Music and Recordings*

Sheet music of each mantra discussed in this book is included on the following pages. It gives full texts, musical notation, and the mantra's purpose. This is intended to help readers unfamiliar with mantras to have a sense of how they can be chanted, and to support musicians in accompanying mantra chanting.

Recordings of *Dhanyavad* (for the joy of gratitude), *Jaya Jaya Devi Mata* (for peace with the mother), and *Om Srim Mahalakshmyai* (for noble wealth) can be found on the Compact Disc included with this book. They are intended to help you feel the mantra's vibration and to invite you to chant along.

Interested readers are referred to our following recordings, which are also listed in the discography.

*Mantras: Magical Songs of Power* (1994) includes seven mantras from this book: *Jaya Jaya Devi Mata* (for peace with the mother), *Hari Om Shiva Om* (for radiant masculine consciousness ), *Om Ham Hanumate* (for healing and strength), *Om Sri Ram Jai Ram Jai Jai Ram* (for victory to the power of love), *Patneem Manoramam Dehi* (to find a female life partner), *Raghupati Raghava Raja Ram* (for triumph of spirit over ego), and *Sat Patim Dehi* (to find a male life partner). In addition it includes eight others: *Panduranga Hari* (for freedom from inhibitions), *Radha Soami Deva Devi* (to communicate with spirits), *Om Asatoma Sadgamaya* (for truth, light, and immortality), *Gopala* (to heal parent/child relationships), *Om Eim Hreem Kleem* (for wisdom, wealth, and protection), *Om Nama Shiva / Adi Shakti* (to harmonize male/female energy), *Ya Devi Sarva Bhuteshu* (for intelligence), and *Om Shanti Om* (for peace).

***Mantras II: To Change Your World*** (1995) includes four mantras from this book: *Dhanyavad* (for the joy of gratitude), *Kodanda Rama / Hara Hara Ganga* (for a miracle), *Om Dum Durgayai / Om Kreem Kaalikayai* (to overcome disease), and *Om Gam Ganapatayae* (to overcome obstacles). In addition it includes four others: *Gate Gate* (for enlightenment), *Saraswathi Mahalakshmi* (for creativity, wealth, and safety), *Shakti Shakti Dhanyavad* (for female power), and *Shivam Shantamidyam* (for peace and protection).

***Mantras III: A Little Bit of Heaven*** (1998) includes *Om Srim Mahalakshmyai* (for noble wealth) from this book. It also includes seven other mantras: *Amba Amba* (for protection of children), *Satyanarayani* (for a happy relationship), *Om Dhiyo Yonaha Prachodayat* (for intuition), *Om Satyam Shivam Sundaram* (for truth, love, and beauty), *Rama Lakshmana Janaki* (for oneness), *Om Namo Bhagavate* (to experience the presence of the divine), and *Om Trayambakam* (to overcome fear of death).

Please remember that pages of music only indicate the vibrations of mantras the way a map indicates a beautiful piece of countryside. Recordings evoke the vibrations and can transport you into the mantra's magical landscape. An experienced teacher can guide you to make your own explorations. I suggest you listen to the mantras being chanted, feel their vibrations, and chant them yourself.

# Dhanyavad

*For the joy of gratitude,*
*to forgive*

Melody and text –
Henry Marshall

Dhanya_vad___  Dhanya__vad___

Dhanya__vad___  A___nan_da__

Dhanya__vad___  Dhanya___vad

Dhanya___vad__  A___nan__da__

# Hari Om Shiva Om

*For radiant masculine consciousness*

Melody and text – Henry Marshall

Hari     Om_____     Shiva     Om__

Shiva     Om__     Hari     Om_____

Hari     Shiva     Shiva     Hari     Om

# *Jaya Jaya Devi Mata*

*For peace with the mother*

Melody and text –
Henry Marshall

Ja_ ya    Ja_ ya    De_ vi    Ma_ ta

Na_____ma_____ha_____

Ja_ ya    Ja_ ya__    De_ vi__    Ma_ ta

Na_____ma_____ha_____

# Kodanda Rama / Hara Hara Ganga

*To protect,*
*to receive a miracle*

Melodies and texts – Sant Keshavadas
Arranged and adapted
by Henry Marshall

Kodanda Rama Pahi    Kodanda Rama

Pattabhi__rama Pahi    Pattabhi__ra____ma

Hara Hara    Ganga    Shiva Shiva    Ganga

Shankara    Ganga    Jai Pandu___ran__ga

# *Om Dum Durgayai / Om Kreem Kaalikayai*

*To overcome negativity, disease, and insomnia*

Melody – Sant Keshavadas,
Henry Marshall, Rickie Moore
Traditional text adapted
by Henry Marshall

Om Dum Durga____ yai    Na___ma___

__ha_____    Om Kreem  Kaa_li__ka___

_ yai_____    Na_ma____ha_____

# Om Gam Ganapatayae

*To begin anything,*
*to overcome obstacles,*
*to have success*

Melody and text – Sant Keshavadas
Arranged and adapted
by Henry Marshall

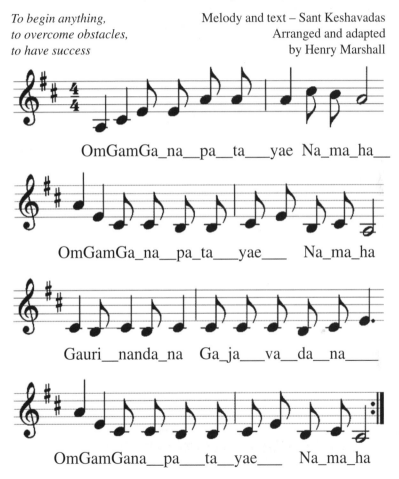

OmGamGa_na__pa__ta___yae Na_ma_ha__

OmGamGa_na__pa_ta___yae___ Na_ma_ha

Gauri__nanda_na Ga_ja___va_da__na____

OmGamGana__pa___ta__yae___ Na_ma_ha

# *Om Ham Hanumate*

*For healing and strength*

Melody – Henry Marshall
and Rickie Moore
Traditional text

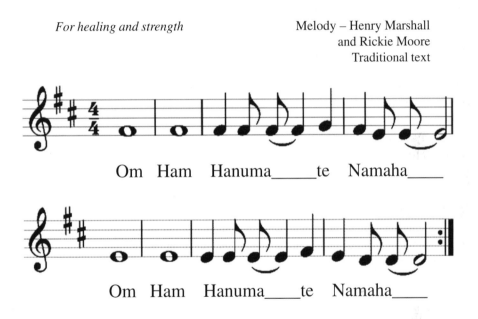

Om  Ham  Hanuma____te  Namaha____

Om  Ham  Hanuma____te  Namaha____

# *Om Sri Ram Jai Ram Jai Jai Ram*

*For victory to*
*the power of love*

Melody – Sant Keshavadas
Traditional text

Om Sri Ram Jai Ram Jai Jai Ram Om

Sri Ram Jai Ram Jai Jai Ram Om

Sri Ram Jai Ram Jai Jai Ram Om

Sri Ram Jai Ram Jai Jai Ram

# *Om Srim Mahalakshmyai*

*For noble wealth*

Melody – Henry Marshall
Traditional text

Om Srim  Ma_ha__lak_____shmyai_____

Na_____ma_____ha_____

Om Srim  Ma_ha_lak_____shmyai   Na _ ma

ha_____

# Patneem Manoramam Dehi

*To find a female
life-partner*

Melody – Henry Marshall
and Rickie Moore
Traditional text

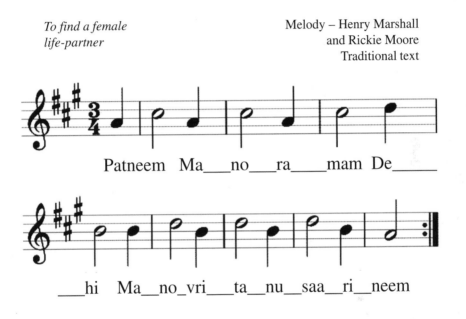

Patneem  Ma___no___ra____mam  De_____

___hi  Ma__no_vri___ta__nu__saa__ri__neem

# *Raghupati Raghava Raja Ram*

*For triumph of*
*spirit over ego*

Traditional melody and text
Adapted by Henry Marshall

Raghupa__ti   Raghava   Ra__ja   Ram

Pa_ti_ta   Pa_va_na   Si_ta_____ram

Raghupati   Raghava   Ra__ja   Ram

Pa_ti_ta   Pa_va_na   Si_ta_____ram

# *Sat Patim Dehi*

*To find a male
life-partner*

Melody – Henry Marshall
and Rickie Moore
Traditional text

Sat Pa___tim    De___hi   Para___meshva

___ra  Sat Pa__tim  De__hi   Para___meshva__ra

# *Appendix B*

## *Pronunciation and Glossary*

| | Pronounce as in | | | Pronounce as in |
|---|---|---|---|---|
| **a** | yog**a** | | **l** | **l**ove |
| **aa** | **aa**rdvark | | **m** | **m**other |
| **ae** | ma**e**lstrom | | **n** | **n**oble |
| **ai** | w**ai**t | | **o** | **o**pen |
| **<u>ai</u>** | **ai**sle | | **oo** | r**oo**m |
| **ay** | w**ay** | | **p** | **p**ot |
| **<u>ay</u>** | **ay**e | | **r** | German **r**uhig |
| **bh** | a**bh**ore | | **s** | **s**ave |
| **dh** | a**dh**ere | | **sh** | **sh**e |
| **e** | w**e**ight | | **t** | **t**op |
| **ee** | n**ee**d | | **th** | an**th**ill |
| **ei** | **Ei**nstein | | **u** | ill**u**minate |
| **g** | **g**ive | | **v** | **v**ision |
| **i** | m**i** | | **w** | **w**ell |
| **j** | **j**oy | | **y** | **y**es |

*A-'nan-da* = bliss

*'Bhak-ti* = the yoga of love

*'Dhan-ya-,vad* = blessed thanks

*'Dhar-ma-raj* = king of righteous action and sacred duty

*'Dum* = seed syllable for protection from any form of danger

*'Dur-ga* = *'Dur-ga-yai* = Goddess/power of invincible protection

*'Ga-ja-va-da-na* = Elephant-headed one

*'Ga-na-,pa-ta-yae* = *Ga-'ne-sha* = Lord of all beings; son of Gauri and Shiva

*'Gam* = seed syllable for overcoming obstacles and for new beginnings

*'Gan-ga* = the sacred river Ganges

*'Gau-ri* = the fair one; mother of Ganesh; wife of Shiva

*'Ham* = seed syllable for healing throat, lungs and immune system

*'Ha-nu-man* = *'Ha-nu-ma-te* = magical monkey devotee of Rama

*'Ha-ra* = power of devastation; remover; giver of wonders

*'Ha-ri* = ray of light; radiant, godly; remover of sin; refers to Vishnu

*'Jai* = *'Jay-a* = victory, alleluia

*,Kaa-'li-ka-yai* = Goddess/power of destruction of evil; Kali

*'Ke-sha-va-,das* = servant of the Lord

*,Ko-'dan-da* = the mighty bow of Rama

*,Ma-ha-'lak-shmi* = *,Ma-ha-'lak-shmy-ai* = Goddess/power of abundance

*Ma-'no-ra-man* = enchanting

*Ma-no-vrit-'ta-nu-,saa-ri-,neem* = proper wishes; established desires

*'Man-tra* = words of power; from "manas" (consciousness ) + "tra" (protection)

*'Ma-ta* = mother

*'Nam* = name; identity

*'Na-ma-ha* = salutations

*Na-'mo* = salutations; name; identity

*'Om* = the cosmic vibration that is the source of all manifestation

*'Pa-hi* = protection

*Pat-'ta-bhi* = coronated

*,Pan-du-'ran-ga* = God as white light

*,Pa-ra-'mesh-vara* = supreme Lord; highest expression of divinity
*Pa-'teem* = husband
*'Pa-,ti-ta* = downtrodden ones
*Pat-,neem* = wife
*'Pa-va-na* = uplift
*'Rag-hu-,pa-ti ,Rag-ha-va* = descendent of the very evolved solar race
*'Ra-ja* = king; noble
*'Ram = 'Ra-ma* = incarnation of Vishnu as noble, loving, righteous king
*'Sat-,gu-ru* = true guru ; noble dispeller of darkness
*'Sant* = saint
*'Sat = 'Sat-ya* = truth, true, noble
*'Sat Nam* = the name is truth; truth is the identity
*'Shi-va* = consciousness (intrinsically masculine) of God; destroyer of evil
*'Si-ta* = wife of Rama; incarnation of Mahalakshmi (goddess of abundance)
*'Sri* = power; refers to Sita/Mahalakshmi, the power (shakti) of Rama/Vishnu
*'Tan-tra* = yoga of transcendence through sexuality , the framework of all life
*'Vish-nu* = God as preserver; the supreme Self
*'Yo-ga* = union; science of neutralizing the alternations of consciousness

| | |
|---|---|
| ' | marks syllable with primary stress |
| , | marks syllable with secondary stress |
| - | marks syllable division |

130

# *Discography*

*Mantras: Magical songs of power.* Henry Marshall and the Playshop Family (1994). Oreade Music: 2MC: ORS 29422AB. 2CD: ORS 29425AB.

   *Mantras II: To change your world.* Henry Marshall and the Playshop Family (1995). Oreade Music: 1MC ORS 52014, 1CD ORS 52012.

   *Mantras III: A little bit of heaven .* Henry Marshall and the Playshop Family (1998). Oreade Music: 1MC ORS 55704, 1CD ORS 55702.

## *Available from:*

*North America*
Bluestar Communications
ph: 800-6-BLUESTAR (800-625-8378), fax: 650-851 2339
email: orders@bluestar.com
internet: http://www.bluestar.com

*Rest of the World*
Oreade music
ph: +31-23-5483535, fax: +31-23-5282500
email: oreade@wxs.nl
internet: http://www.oreade.com

# *Bibliography*

Bergstrom, G. *Diamond body*. Tucson: Bergstrom, 1996.

_____*Butterflies need no taxidermist*. Tucson: Bergstrom, 1997.

Gore, A. *Earth in the balance*. New York: Houghton Mifflin, 1992.

Huxley, A. *The doors of perception and Heaven and hell*. New York: Harper and Row, 1954.

Leary, T. *Personal communication to the author*. September 9, 1975. In Marshall, H. *In search of Timothy Leary: A psychohistorical biography*. Unpublished doctoral dissertation. Knoxville: University of Tennessee, 1976.

_____*Interpersonal diagnosis of personality: A functional theory and methodology for personality evaluation*. New York: Ronald Press, 1957.

Leary, T., Metzner, R., and Alpert, R. *The psychedelic experience*. New Hyde Park: University Books, 1964.

Keshavadas, S. S. *This is wisdom*. Oakland: Temple of Cosmic Religion, 1975.

_____*Cosmic shakti kundalini (the universal mother): A devotional approach*. Detroit: Harlo, 1976a.

_____*Ramayana at a glance*. Oakland: Temple of Cosmic Religion, 1976b. Companion recording: *Tulisidas Ramayana*.

_____*Stories and parables*. New York: Vantage Press, 1979.

_____*Healing techniques of the holy east*. Oakland: Temple of Cosmic Religion, 1980. Companion recording: *Healing mantras of the holy east*.

Radha, S. *Mantras: Words of power*. Spokane: Timeless Books, 1994.

Tigunait, P. *The power of mantra and the mystery of initiation* Honesdale: Yoga International Books, 1996.

Yogananda, P. *Self-realization fellowship lessons*. Los Angeles: SRF, 1956.
_____ *Autobiography of a yogi*. Los Angeles: SRF 1968.

# *Credits*

The author is grateful for permission to reprint the photographs on the following pages.

Page 14: Marshall family
Page 19: H. Marshall
Page 21: Attributed to Katie Coast by Mary Emily Barret Marshall
Page 25: The Flight, 1967, Jesuit High School, Shreveport, Louisiana
Page 34: Skipworth Studios, Shreveport, Louisiana
Page 44: H. Marshall
Page 55: Friends on Temple of Cosmic Religion Pilgrimage
Page 67: Beam of Eros XXVII, © Sharon Stewart
Page 84: Friends at Temple of Cosmic Religion ceremony
Page 91: Nancy Moore
Page 95: Frank Berger
Page 97: Spiegelbeeld Magazine
Page 136: Horacio Sormani
Back cover: R. Moore
Cover photos: compliment of PhotoDisc, Inc.
All other photographs: compliment of PhotoDisc, Inc.

Rickie Moore and Henry Marshall

# *About the Author*

## *by Rickie Moore, Ph.D.*

When I first met Henry, he had his doctorate, had taught at two universities, was consulting at four hospitals and forty schools, and worked primarily with disadvantaged children. But beneath the traditional white coat of the clinical psychologist, I sensed something special. I was curious if he was as he seemed: a lover of humanity and devotee of truth. Now, after living with him for many years, I know he is a real, practical man, who is gentle and compassionate; a man who can cry, play, and parent; a liberated man who protects and appreciates powerful women; a real hero, who does not fell trees, but plants them. I have been privileged to witness the often-amazing results of Henry's talents. Through his openness and determination he integrates ancient Eastern teachings with modern Western behavioral science. Through the magic of mantras, he helps people realize their dreams. I know, I am his wife.

138

# *For more information*

For more information about mantras or Inner Peace Playshops, please contact the author at one of the following addresses:

web site:
*http://www.euronet.nl/~inpeace*

Email:
*inpeace@euronet.nl*

mail:
*Mantras—A musical path to peace*
*P.O. Box 14546*
*1001 LA Amsterdam*
*The Netherlands*

# *Index*